From The Command Car

From The Command Car

UNTOLD STORIES OF THE 628TH
TANK DESTROYER BATTALION
WITNESSED FIRST-HAND AND
TOLD BY CHARLES A. LIBBY, TEC 5
OFFICIAL COMMAND CAR DRIVER

* * *

Steve Hunter

Copyright © 2015 Steve Hunter
All rights reserved.

ISBN: 0692512411
ISBN 13: 9780692512418

Dedication

As the interviewer and author of this untold history of WWII, I would like to dedicate this book to the following people. First, I wish to express my deepest thanks to Mr. Charles A. Libby for this opportunity to hear his incredible stories and to give me the honor of bringing them to life on paper to the many readers who will enjoy them as I have during these past years of interviews and appearances on this important topic. It is my sincere desire that they will be preserved for future generations to enjoy and learn from.

In these past years of knowing Mr. Libby, I have listened to many stories of his time served in the European Theater of Operations during World War II. This time in history helped to shape and define the world as we know it today. It is most certainly an honor and a personal joy to have associated with and listened to one of the men who actually aided in that great effort.

I wish to thank his entire family for their faith in me and their blessings of confidence to tackle this very important and special project with their beloved father, especially his sons Chuck and Rob Libby and his daughter Deb Lehman who initially asked me for their father to take this project with their trust and their blessings.

Thank you to my wife Alma and my daughters, Michelle and Angelina for operating the video camera as we filmed these initial interviews to also capture these stories on film. Your patience and understanding is appreciated during this time of extensive work on this book.

Special thanks also goes out to James Hunter Dortman for his research assistance during the writing of this book in a few areas of difficulty, a young man that sees the importance of this book and enjoyed the time spent listening to Mr. Libby as he told his stories.

I would also like to thank and dedicate this manuscript to all of the soldiers who served during this *war to end all wars*, for their tremendous sacrifices they made. Giving life and limbs to overcome the evil that plagued the world, our soldiers in every uniform on the many battlefields are all heroes who must forever be remembered! Each story told is historical truth and should pave the way to new knowledge about WWII and better help to prevent the repeating of similar events which caused great pain, anguish, unbelievable atrocities, terror and so many unnecessary deaths. Knowledge is power and should be used to better the human race and not used to destroy it. It is our responsibility to teach this present generation and all that will follow, about these great men and women and their remarkable accomplishments as well as their many unselfish sacrifices. We must always remember them and always be thankful for this brave generation of warriors. In a time where Americans have very thin skin and are offended by every detail that unfolds in front of them through ignorance and political greed, history itself is being removed and in some cases, destroyed right in front of our eyes. This book does not pull it's punches or try to add fluff and desensitized writing methods. It is the truth spoken from a man that lived it in an effort to preserve history as it unfolded. So with that said, "God bless each one of them and God Bless the United States of America"!

Last, but not least, I would like to give glory to my Lord and Savior, Jesus Christ for the ability to prepare this manuscript and for the many promises of life that I will have in Heaven. Thank you Lord for guiding me and placing such wonderful people into my life.

On behalf of Mr. Charles A. Libby, he would like to dedicate the stories of this book and to the memory of all the soldiers of the 628th Tank Destroyer Battalion who he had the honor of serving with during this time in our history. Special thanks go out to the great men of the C-Company for which he was a proud member during this world conflict for the lifetime of memories.

He would also like to thank the many people who worked so tirelessly in the CCC Camps of Pennsylvania. Mr. Libby has expressed the great value of these camps and how they helped to shape his future, his work ethics and his entire way of living.

He adds that these stories are a part of our American history and it is his life's wish that they are not lost. It is also his wish that his entire family have a written record of what their loving father, grandfather and great-grandfather did while serving in the greatest armed forces tank unit and in his own words, *"the greatest group of men that ever lived."*

He also wishes to thank his entire family for their support and all the loving care they provide to him on a daily basis. He concludes his dedication with . . . "God bless and I hope that you enjoy my stories that I experienced in WWII *"From the Command Car."*

Acknowledgment

✶ ✶ ✶

The incredible stories of the boys who served, fought and died to rid the world of evil during WWII, in the spoken words of TEC 5 C-Company Command Car driver,

Charles A. Libby

and his recall of serving in the 628th Tank Destroyer Battalion.

Table of Contents

Acknowledgment ix
Prologue xiii
My Roots in Pennsylvania 1
The Civilian Conservation Corps Camps 19
Enlistment, Basics and My Unit 47
Shipping Out – Europe, Here We Come! 74
Our Weapons and Gear 84
Our Path to the Germans 97
The Letter of Protection 189
Occupation of Europe 194
Death in Many Forms 217
Home Sweet Home 223
The Men Who Fought 234
Later in Life 237
Two WWII Veterans Meet 252
A Note and Disclaimer from the Author 257
About the Author 261
Sponsors Of History 263

Prologue

✱ ✱ ✱

THE WORLD SEEMED AS IF it was upside down with many American families in dire need of some form of divine intervention. People were hungry and living with little money and almost no hope in a time of absolute turmoil. As if life here at home wasn't hard enough, by just a boat trip across the Atlantic Ocean, evil with it's sharpened talons and it's fangs of hatred had reared its ugly head and systematically spread out across the entire continent of Europe. While here in America, a strong sense of patriotism and unity sprouted within us as a nation with the overwhelming desire and need to right what was being wronged. These feelings spread across the nation much like an uncontrollable wildfire in the sun-dried forests of the northwest United States. With a sense of utter desperation on the home front and the reality of either starving during our country's great depression or the fearful possibility of having foreign troops on our home soil, the men and women of this great nation stepped up to the unified call and collectively prevented a rabid mad man on his glutinous rampage from controlling Europe, it's neighbors and possibly the entire modern world.

Our normal lives as we knew it and the peace and harmony of every nation which existed at the time, was put on hold as good and evil faced off in what was to be known as *"the war that was to end all wars."* Their armies, consisting of brain-washed men and children alike, were led by a tyrant who still to this very day is compared to Satan himself. An evil group of well-armed and well-funded tyrants literally became an enemy to not just uniformed soldiers, but the entire human race itself. Years of well-planned and methodical terror, prejudice, killing, raping and looting to satisfy an unquenchable thirst for the perfect race of people and the goals of complete control of populations, marked a place in world history that almost saw the end of an entire generation and race of God's chosen and special people.

To say that Adolph Hitler was anything other than pure evil in human form would be a great understatement to say the least. His desires and well thought out plan to eliminate those who were not up to the standards of his *perfect society*, are still discussed and studied today by students, historians and psychologists alike to find some form of rational thinking for his inhumane and unbelievable actions. A constant study still exists of how he even got as far as he did with the entire world not even blinking an eye until his army of *marching zombies* began to file across Germany to invade its peaceful neighbors. Unseen by this generation of human kind, a methodical plan was now in action to align with the weak, to use their manpower and wealth for their benefit, strengthen its overall numbers, destroy everything in its path and to continue spreading out in every possible direction to gain strength. This omnidirectional attack was like that of a vine wrapping itself around a majestic tree and slowly squeezing the life out of its roots. A strangling vine that caused pain by killing and destroying everything within its path, making claim to whatever it found as precious and of importance to the sickening cause and undeniable greed of the self-proclaimed commander, Adolph Hitler.

America fully enters the war in Europe after Japanese *Kamikaze* pilots attack Pearl Harbor, Hawaii. The Imperial Japanese aligned with the Germans, force the hand of the American government and all of her military power and put its skills to the test. Young men begin to enlist in record numbers prior to others being drafted into military service. Patriotism sprouts its own vines and begins to grow and flourish into an intricate network of US military might. Help was needed in many parts of the world as America joins with her allies and begins one of the greatest military strategies of all time as they attack and engage the Axis Powers, as they soon became known to the rest of the world.

Our nation's leaders wrestle with thoughts of what these men would face as they confront this great enemy. Our military commanders and president alike also wonder if they would be physically tough enough or have enough military might to defeat an already deeply entrenched army. More importantly, would they be mentally tough enough to handle the many horrors and atrocities that they may face for the first time in their very young lives? To be transplanted onto another continent across the world, far away from the comforts of home and to seek out and destroy a *killing machine*, would be something that any human being would never had dreamed they would be faced with in their lifetime where boys would become men and many others, ghosts. Either way, our country was in it for the duration and there was never any thought of turning back. This was World War II and it seemed at the time, to the many that saw it and lived it, the start of the foretold prophecy of the end of the world!

With the overwhelming feeling of fear and literally being backed into a corner much like a trapped and injured animal, we faced a time where as a country, we needed to do incredible things. One would be to arm an entire nation to the hilt and establish ourselves as a superior fighting force that no other country could match themselves against. Another, would most certainly have to be our superior technological advances and how they would need to come into play during this conflict. Finally, and most importantly, the *true grit American spirit* of our fighting men which was like no other fighting force ever known. Our very appearance as a *snarling tiger* and our well-planned battle attacks would prove too much for the German armies to overcome.

Our support and patriotic duty here in the homeland placed ordinary Americans alike in crucial jobs to help aid in the war effort. The *"Rosy the Riveter"* concept, the purchasing of war bonds to help the government's effort's financially with the overwhelming costs of war and the conservation and donation of precious metals to be converted into workable product for tools and weapons which we needed abroad, were all tremendous sacrifices from each and every American citizen. These were all massive puzzle pieces where through pride and patriotism, sweat and blood, were all fit together to complete a grand picture of *VICTORY!*

Charles A. Libby was just one of those many puzzle pieces. His contributions as a member of the 628th Tank Destroyer Battalion weren't heard on the radio or thought of as extraordinary in any of today's history books, but they were very important none-the-less! Each and every person that wore the uniform of our armed services played an important role in some way which helped to complete this *"puzzle of victory."* As a command car driver in C-Company of the 628th, Charles A. Libby performed and witnessed first-hand many heroic deeds, acts of courage and worthy accomplishments which have never been told in print before now. With the complete generation of WWII veterans leaving us daily at an increasing rate and the last bit of first–hand information about this war disappearing, Mr. Libby wanted to make sure that the *information puzzle* wasn't left incomplete when it came to the 628th. So, with this manuscript, he hopes that these brave soldiers are properly honored and never forgotten as he shares these stories about the men which he fought beside, bonded with and witnessed perform many amazing feats. With some humorous details, shocking admissions and truths from behind the scenes in the constant company of the C-Company commanders, Charles opens up his mind to all the memories which he has kept locked away for over seventy years. A new twist on many historical events of WWII, recall of its main battles and the opinions of a man that heard commands handed down from HQ and how decisions were made to send soldiers into harm's way and how he miraculously came away from every major battle he faced without as much as a scratch while serving his country, *"From the Command Car."*

My Roots in Pennsylvania

✳ ✳ ✳

THE *KEYSTONE STATE* OF PENNSYLVANIA is where this tribute story begins. The tall, lush pine trees and oaks of the Allegheny Mountains line the many streams and creeks of this branch of the mighty Susquehanna River. An industrious lumber community and picture perfect landscape which marks the stomping grounds for any young boy's dream upbringing. For my subject, a life of simple existence and a fairly normal childhood of the day and age growing up in this particular section of the North Eastern United States.

The son of Theodore and Laura Jane Libby, Charles Ardell Libby was born in the city of Williamsport, Pennsylvania on October 3, 1917, during the Woodrow Wilson presidential administration. Born at The Williamsport Hospital, Charles Libby was of Irish descent with each parent being the son and daughter of first generation immigrants to this great country. Charles's grand-parents eagerly passed through the long and arduous lines at New York's Ellis Island to seek out a better way of life here in America. His grandfather Libby proudly brought ten children into the world in Weichert, Pennsylvania, a small town near the Selinsgrove area. Passing away at the early age of 42, shortly after being a victim of a scam or as Mr. Libby describes as being *flim-flammed*, a con artist took away his claims and financial rights to an iron ore mine which would had provided a good living for the entire family for many years to come as well as a great degree of family wealth. A hard lesson to be learned when coming here to this country with the aspirations of providing a better living for his family. Having never had the opportunity to meet his grandfather, it seems to have left an empty spot in Charles's childhood memories. He did however have the good fortune and blessed opportunity to meet his grandmother Libby in his early years, who he describes fondly as a very fine Christian woman.

A young Charles Libby seated third from left, back row, with Elementary School classmates.

Known to most of his childhood friends as Chuck and sometimes Ardell by the pranksters and teasers of the neighborhood attempting to wake him up from his bedroom window, Charles Libby lived a seemingly normal existence with pretty much the same start in life and childhood upbringing as many of the young boys at that time in central Pennsylvania. Although, being born at a hospital and not in the home was found to be unusual and a type of healthcare luxury that many women weren't often privileged to or provided during childbirth, Charles A. Libby got his start in a sterile environment which may or may not had contributed to the lack of germs, disease and other elements that were very much present during this time in our country's history. This start may had affected his survival and certainly that of his mother's. He certainly has proven that since his birth, longevity and overall good health throughout his life has always been present. At the ripe age of 97 years old during these interviews and the writing of this manuscript, Charles A. Libby is still very physically active and also demonstrates a tremendous recall of these written events that occurred during his time served in the European Theater of WWII. And now, as the oldest member of his family and with no other living relatives other than his children and the children of his brother and sisters as well as several grandchildren and great-grandchildren, Charles feels a deep personal responsibility to pass this information onto them, not only about the stories of war, but also about their proud Libby family history.

Mr. Libby recalls some of his favorite childhood memories and how he played hard all the time from skillfully swinging and hanging on the school monkey bars to getting his clothes dirty down on the banks of the Susquehanna River. The river seemed to be one of the places that he spent most of his time. Becoming quite a strong swimmer, the young Charles even rescued a girl from the swift waters of the Loyalsock Creek as she nearly drowned in front of her parents.

> "I saw her bobbing up and down and then didn't come up too fast. I swam to her as fast as I could and pulled her up out of the water by her hair! She gasped for air and spit out the creek water as I started to swim toward the shore to get her to safety. She turned to me and grabbed me tightly in a bear hug and I could barely swim. When I got close to the shore where I could stand up, I just let go of her. She was able to stand then as well and come around from her scare. Her parents were near by and thanked me. She was lucky that I was there to save her or it would have been very bad for her and her parents."

A sixty foot bridge in the area over the river also added excitement for the young Charles Libby. With the swimming skills added to the fact that he had no fear as a young man, Charles would perform a flawless *swan dive* off of this bridge, all the time yelling much like *Tarzan*! This story was also documented to me in these final stages of writing the manuscript from family that used to swim with him who stated that he was very skilled and was the only one that would do this particular dive from that great height.

Mr. Libby also recalls some of the more popular games played with his neighborhood buddies like playing baseball or sneaking into the local theater to see a free silent movie which at the time would cost five or ten cents while watching a local resident play the piano while the movie ran. This feature added to the excitement of the film which in turn made up for the fact that it was shown without any sound.

Remembering many of these old films fondly and smiling at the likes of Charlie Chaplin and quietly laughing when recalling being scared at films like The Phantom of The Opera and Boris Karloff's Frankenstein character, Mr. Libby's memories of these times are much like yesterday. The Keystone Cops also provided a comical memory as they drove down the road in a sped up motion as the engine dropped right out of the bottom of their car. Following their moment of precise comical timing and unfortunate circumstances, they all get out, picked up the engine, threw it in the back seat and drove off leaving theater goers, like the young Charles Libby, laughing hysterically. He also remembers the first movies that depicted the failed flights of the famous Wright Brothers. Snickering about the planes flipping over and the footage of how they kept trying before they finally succeeded, Mr. Libby proudly remarks that he saw the history of flight from the very start and then eventually a man being blasted into space. Charles was fortunate to be living in a unique generation of rapid growth and technological advancements that only a man of his advanced age would have had the chance to see and experience.

Other favorite childhood activities were hiking up Bald Eagle Mountain as well as hanging out by the local dam and various swimming holes. Being strong and brave enough to swim completely across the wide Susquehanna river at one clip, Charles takes pride in the fact that he was always in great shape and took great care of his body. As a child, Charles recalls that he knew the river's currents well enough to help emergency rescue teams find a young boy who had drown in some of its rougher waters. While these rescue teams where looking for a young boy out in the center area of the river, young Charles instructed the many volunteers and rescue personal to search in a particular area where they were able to find the lifeless body from his exact instructions. Just a start of the long line of remarkable and unselfish deeds that Mr. Libby would speak about while being interviewed for this manuscript.

The most daring and dangerous of his early activities was known as *train jumping*. At the age of fourteen or fifteen, armed with only a pocket knife, wooden matches and a hatchet, catching a ride on a local freight train to another town for the day was an adventure he very much enjoyed. Then, as the sun would start to set for the day, getting back to his hometown of Williamsport on another passenger train would be his next big challenge. Sometimes other kids would see them doing this and would join in by following them for the day's adventures. Many times without their parents even knowing where they were, Charles always took great care to protect the younger ones that tagged along, making sure that they got home in one piece. Having heard these tales from my own grandfather, Charles Hunter, a Pennsylvania Railroad engineer, I knew that these stories held water and that it was a popular game with the youngsters of the days as well as the preferred form of transportation for the vagabond travelers known as hobo's, who couldn't afford the railroad's passenger train fares.

Hiding in the bushes along the tracks of the Pennsylvania Railroad to wait for the right moment to jump on-board, the boys would catch the scheduled passenger trains and seek the hiding places within the doorway of a mail car which was located just behind its coal tender car.

The ride was very rough as the train flew at high rates of speed down the old tracks. Each of the boys would hold on for dear life, clinging to the bars outside of the car while being shaken much like that of a rough carnival ride until finally reaching their destination.

The boys would each get off and walk into a small Pennsylavania town known as Watsontown as the train would stop to fill up with water which was needed to produce steam for its engines of the times. Charles remembers one time in particular as they made their way into town being especially hungry. With four mouths to feed this particular day, he instructed the younger ones to go door-to-door to ask the local residents for canned items to put together a *Mulligan Stew*, an Irish favorite. As the boys returned with the days take, Charles found a large empty can that he mixed all of the ingredients into with the addition of clean creek water as he began to mix his Irish-style stew. Cooked over a fire that they boys started with the wooden matches that they always carried in their pockets, on this day they enjoyed a hearty and healthy meal. The best part of the meal Charles recalls is that it was free! The worst part of the meal he recalls was that they had no eating utensils, so the entire meal was eaten with just their bare hands. None-the-less, the meal was still a complement to their already free train ride for the day.

Now, with full bellies, the next problem to solve as Mr. Libby remarked . . .

```
"Now, we were all wondered how we were going
to get back home to Williamsport."
```

The boys walked far above the train station where they believed the engine would make it's next stop or at least slow down. The boys all knew that hese passenger trains would ultimately arrive in Charles's hometown of Williamsport but, if they'd happen to miss the stop, they would end up in Altoona, PA which was over three hours from where they were supposed to be after their full day of excitement. Their choice of positioning was crucial and on this day proved to be correct. Mr. Libby remarked that the engine stopped precisely where they had hidden in the brush to make their move in hopping on one of the cars. Jumping onto the scheduled passenger train, the four boys once again assumed their positions, securely braced themselves for the bumpy ride ahead of them and off they went in the direction of home. Upon their arrival in Williamsport, Charles and his friend Fred Smithgall lifted the younger boys down off of the train. He instructed them to quickly run across the five sets of tracks at this particular station and not to look back as they ran for their homes in an attempt to keep their position a secret if one of the train conductor's had seen them running. . Charles had also told them to tell their parents that they had been playing at the river for the day and simply lost track of time to keep their activity a secret from them as well. A dangerous and yet exciting type of activity admits Mr. Libby, but fortunately by the grace of God, nobody ever had gotten hurt while they were having fun train jumping.

Charles also remembers from his youth the *Black Hand Gang,* who ran most of the city's underground and illegal operations during these hard times by making moonshine and selling their highly desired liquor out the back door of the local theater and many other local businesses within the city.

Being egged-on by his neighborhood buddies to try and get them a bottle of whiskey, Mr. Libby remembers knocking on one of those doors with only twenty five cents in his pocket, which they all scraped together for this *hail marry* attempt at getting some moonshine alcohol. During prohibition, a black market bottle of whiskey would cost interested parties fifty cents. Now, here was a young Charles Libby, of Irish decent, knocking on a door in a dark alley of the notorious Italian Black Hand Gang, trying to buy whiskey for young boys and only having half of the amount that was being demanded at that time. Mr. Libby recalls that he knocked at the door and boldly told the man that he knew what was going on there and that he would tell the local cops about them, *unless* he could buy a fifth of whiskey. The large man that had opened the door looked down at the cocky young Irish boy and told him that he was a little brat, as he attempted to close the door in his face. As Charles quickly stuck his foot in the doorway, the now panicing man frantically told him to get his foot out of the doorway. Mr. Libby still remembers with a big smile on his face the moment that he was looking at this man once again and telling him that he would tell the cops if he didn't sell him the whiskey that he and his neighborhood friends wanted. Reluctantly, the man had no other choice and was forced to open the door and allow the young and bold Charles to enter. Knowing that their entire operation was at stake of being ratted out by a twelve year old boy, the man reluctantly sold Charles a pint of whiskey, at his requested discounted price. After that, all the other neighborhood boys knew that if they wanted to get booze from the Black Hand Gang, Charles was the guy to get it for them, but for a price of course. This was just one of the ways that Charles took those desperate times and turned it into a small enterprising business operation to help out his family, as well as having some of his own spending money in his pocket for candy and the movies. Sounds like something right out of a Little Rascals episode with a slightly rated R twist. As time went on and trust was built between this notorious gang and Charles, he sometimes acted as a lookout for their illegal operations. He remembers the times of alerting them to the police passing by and then giving the all clear to the men as they were far enough away to resume their underground booze business during this time of prohibition. With one of those grins on his face, he takes a moment to tuck the story back into his memories and moves right along into the next tale of his childhood with the comment of . . .

> "They didn't have a choice of selling me the booze. I was young and hard-headed. Whatever I wanted as a kid, I knew that I was going to try hard and would get it."

Also remembering fondly as a young boy, Charles recalls the times spent with his family and friends around the AM radio to get their daily news. Mr. Libby makes note of hearing such famous reports of the times as the Lindbergh baby being kidnapped, the Jack Dempsey fights with Gene Tunney and John Sullivan as well as the capture of the notorious bank robbers known as Bonnie and Clyde.

> "I made over five bucks after the news was reported by selling the local paper on my

```
route the night they announced the kidnap-
ping of the Lindbergh baby. People couldn't
get the newspaper fast enough and I sold
all I had been given to sell. That was very
good money for those times, especially for
a young kid!"
```

The music of the times played on the radio featured singers like Al Jolson and others which Charles loved to dance to, an especially favorite activity of Charles having learned how to do the cha-cha and the assorted waltz's to the smooth sounding music of the times. This was very appealing to the young Charles as he worked hard perfecting his dancing skills at The Park Ballroom. This activity and special hobby has stretched far into his adulthood and still does to this very day. He also noted that when he started dancing, that it was a serious thing to him and it helped him to get away from all the kid's stuff and the many things that may had gotten him into serious trouble like buying booze from the local gangs and moonshiners. Becoming skilled in the variety of dances of the day gave Charles had a new-found confidence within himself and with the ladies that he would lead around the dance floor. Now at 97 years old, Mr. Libby still makes it out at least two to three times a week to dance with the ladies in his hometown, keeping his body active and always reliving the very fond memories of his younger days spent learning this enjoyable art form. Having being compared to the Australian-born, American film actor Errol Flynn in his younger days with many of the same striking features, Charles wooed the ladies on the many dance floors he stepped onto and found it an easy and enjoyable way to start conversation with each one of them.

Mr. Libby often talks fondly of his family, especially his parents. His father, Theodore Thomas Libby, provided the needs of his family by working as an all-around wood carpenter. He speaks highly of his father who worked hard to give him what he truly needed in life well into his seventies. Working on roofs and other dangerous conditions forced his employer to let the elder Mr. Libby go with great sadness in his later years of age. Again, with great appreciation for his father, at this point Charles Libby wanted to help his family even more. With a Bible that his father kept by his bedside, his faith and only being out of work for less than a year, Theodore Libby bounced back and got a job as a maintenance man at the very same hospital in which his son Charles was born and worked hard there until his natural death at 84 years old. The man who gave his father this position, Jack Cardine, was someone that Charles knew from the area and also ran into while in France during his time serving in WWII. Mr. Libby recalls that he may have had a little something to do with his father getting the job from this man's mutual respect for his military service while overseas.

With deep regret and sadness, Mr. Libby expresses the relationship between himself and his father as being good, but not the closeness that he would had liked to have felt as many young boys and fathers often experience in life. With the welling of tears in his eyes, he wishes that many years ago he had told his father to his face that he loved him, leaving a type of black cloud over his head for his entire adulthood. He does recall that his father was very proud of what his son did for his family in the many ways which Charles helped them and America itself during his service in the war. Mr. Libby remembers that his father would often ask him to dress in his formal military uniform after he returned from Europe so that his many friends could see his son looking official. Theodore would beam with pride as the local residents of their neighborhood asked him many questions and proudly shook his hand. Not the hand of the boy they once knew, but now the hand that went off to war and came back a man's. Charles also felt great pride in what he had done and vividly remembers his father telling others that this was his son that served with General Patton. At that point in Charles's life, he actually felt that his father not only loved his son, but also respected him as a man for what he had done.

Mr. Libby painfully remembers sitting in the hallway hearing the sounds coming from the hospital room of his father fighting until the end of his life at the ripe old age of eighty four. As he recalls and speaks of this particular memory, once again with many tears welling up in his eyes he comments on that sad moment in time.

```
"Fluid and kidney infection, that's what did
him in. Boy, he didn't want to die. He put
up a good fight! I could hear him in there
in his hospital bed yelling that he wasn't
going to die. He kept this up until he fi-
nally passed on. My father was always good
to me, I can't complain about him at all."
```

Mr. Libby indicated that his mother, Laura Libby, was a soft spoken Christian woman whose family came from Ithaca, New York. Laura's father, Clarence McManigal, was a tool and die maker by trade. He recalls an early childhood memory of visiting him once at his personal workshop to see what he did there. Impressed with this trade at an early age, Mr. Libby fondly remembers that his grandfather was very talented and worked a very hard to make an honest living.

His mother Laura traveled all the way to Baltimore, Maryland to say goodbye to her beloved father while on his death bed. Charles's uncle drove her there to see her father one last time. Mr. Libby was not present but was told that during this last visit Clarence was flat on his back in that final stage of his life and just before taking his final breath, he rose upright in the bed, looked at his daughter Laura and said aloud, "*Lau, you should see these blue and white beautiful roads.*" He looked at his daughter Laura, smiled, lay back and he was on his journey toward those beautiful blue and white roads which he had just been shown by God. Both Charles and his mother alike believed that these were the roads leading into Heaven. This very strong memory has been in Mr. Libby's memories for his entire life and his belief in Heaven and God himself has been reenforced through this powerful event that his grandfather experienced those many years ago.

Another very strong memory of his mother was that she knew the Bible very well. One memory that does escape Mr. Libby is how his mother and father actually met, but he does recall how strongly they loved each other as man and wife for many years and shared that love until Laura passed away at the ripe old age of seventy six. Laura would often speak to Charles about what the Bible contained and prayed for his well-being and daily safety. He also remembers her often saying to him that there would be days of *trials and tribulations* that he would see later in his life. She once told him that there will be a day that the only way he will be able to tell the seasons is by the leaves on the trees. In our private discussions, Mr. Libby strongly expressed his true feelings that we are quickly approaching this time his mother spoke of and remembers his mother's words as he speaks of her in a softer tone with a half-smile on his face and his eyes looking toward the ground.

> "People better wake up soon and do the right things. The world needs fixed soon!"

Afflicted with a kidney disorder, it was hard for his mother to get out and attend church but found plenty of time between taking care of her family to read and become highly educated in the comforting words and lessons of The Bible. Charles's sister Dorothy was with his mother at the Williamsport Hospital when she passed away from her illness. She later provided this comforting detail to Charles about her passing. Just before her last breath, just as her father had done, she sat up in her bed, looked at Dorothy, smiled and said, "Oh, Roxy, I have so much to tell you!" Roxy was his mother Laura's sister who had passed away long before both Dorothy and Charles were even born. This was just another form of proof to the faithful Libby Family of the existence of a better place which we can go to after death here on earth. Seeing her long-passed sister on her death bed was just another sign that the Libby family has been blessed.

For the Libby family, the Bible was a great source of inspiration and spiritual strength that was needed to survive the many hardships they faced during these particularly trying times during our county's great depression. As the steadfast source of caring and love in the family, Laura did her best with what she had and never complained. Charles's older brother Robert didn't share the same feeling about helping the family which placed more of the weight on Charles himself. Taking any money earned for himself after moving to California and getting a labor job picking fruit on a farm, his older brother would use the money to go into town and have a good time. This never set well with Charles and what he had been taught by his parents on the lesson of helping others. He expressed that he always wondered why his older brother didn't go into the CCC Camps of Pennsylvania or why he didn't join the military service to help out at home and expresses his personal thoughts as such . . .

```
"My brother was good to me and I shouldn't
talk badly about him, but that was how it
was. My dad even put him out of our home once
and my mother would secretly place meals on
the back fence of our yard without my father
knowing to make sure that he at least had
some food to eat for that day."
```

With his mother dressing Charles in his best clothes and button shoes, attending Sunday school at the Christian Church nearby their home was a must in the Libby household. Sending her children off to learn what she found to be true in her heart and to provide them with a strong foundation in God's word which she knew they would carry throughout their adult lives long after she was in Heaven herself, was important to Laura. This was a tradition that Mr. Libby has carried on into the Libby household when he himself started his own family. He and his children still attend church services, studies and activities and often mention the words that his mother taught him more than a half a century ago.

A family of four siblings and two adults to feed was nothing less than a twenty four hour a day chore during the depression for this Pennsylvania family. An older brother and younger sister who both passed away from illness during their infancy, marks two separate sad occasions in which the Libby family would need to count on their strength and personal faith. Never in his wildest dreams imagining that he would be the last of his family to be alive within his generation, especially after serving his country in a World War, Mr. Libby often tells stories and speaks fondly of his siblings and parents alike. In my questioning, I felt to the need to ask him if he thinks that there is a *special* reason why he is the last to live among his family members and to still be here on earth to tell this amazing and unbelievable story. In his truthful and to-the-point fashion, Mr. Libby replied with this story to tell what he believes is the reason why.

> "A friend of mine named Rose, as well as many others who I have known in my later years of my life, have told me that I was blessed. When I asked my minister what that meant for me, he told me that at some time in my life that I did something that somebody else above had recognized as being good."

With further conversation about this matter, Mr. Libby believes that his many good deeds and caring for others in their great time of need, as well as treating others fairly throughout his lifetime, was the reason for this blessed life that he has had and still lives to this day. As I listen to his stories and learn more and more about the man behind the words and stories of this manuscript, I too feel that he has been blessed and is an inspiration to many who meet and personally know him. He is also a man with great integrity and wants others to know how he has endured life with all of it's ups and downs for ninety seven years by faith, honesty and helping others. Not just the ramblings of an old man near death, but the experiences and lessons of an old and wise man that wishes to pass onto others what he has done and how others can do the same to live a blessed life.

In his earlier years of life, Charles attended grade school at the Washington Elementary School on Third St. in Williamsport, Pennsylvania. After completing elementary school, he then moved into Curtain Junior High School, not far away. Charles completed most of the eighth grade and truly enjoyed the classes that they placed him in which offered realistic, hands-on training for jobs that he would probably encounter in the real world. These were the early stages of trade or technical schools, which became popular to those of the times who had difficulty with the academic aspect of the public schools. Again, with tears welling up in his eyes and a hard swallow from the throat, Mr. Libby explains,

> "The depression was going on and things were very serious! My mother told me one time, Charles we're going to have a delicacy tonight, we're going to have bread and milk. She sent me to the local store to buy it for ten cents."

Something needed to be done and Charles was going to do it for his family no matter what it took. Not completely uncommon or unheard of at the time for young men to leave school anywhere from the sixth to eighth grade to go to work and help their families, Charles was one of those statistics To have as many members of the household working and bringing home whatever they could to provide just the most basic of needs, necessary food and to provide a good home and shelter for the large family day in and day out was how it had to be done for many families in this area of the country.

> "I wasn't really doing that great in school. My wood working and machine shop skills were good but my reading wasn't that good. I would pray to God to help me with my reading skills and it just never worked. So, I figured I'd eventually join the CCC Camps when I was old enough and see if I could help out financially at home."

Also, at an early age, Charles's Uncle Dan would come to town from his cabin in Nisbet, Pennsylvania and would bring with him large bundles of what was known as *trailing pine* and *bitter sweet* to sell at the farmer's market in downtown Williamsport. To help his uncle as well as his family to make extra money with little to no overhead, these products were a great way to supplement their income as well as fill a need for this product. Trailing pine was used as the material in making Christmas wreaths and the bitter sweet plant was a type of orange berry which grew wild in the area. These berries were popular decorations to hang on Christmas trees before the mass production of decorations like balls and other Christmas ornaments. Just one more example of the character of the man from a young age that would someday grow into a man who would be asked to help bring down a tyrant that would threaten the entire world. A soldier of necessity and of true compassion for his family to survive these rough times, Charles always found a way. He did what he had to do to help and never complained about the way he had to do it, which was most often through long hours of hard work.

With all of his siblings graduating from High School in their respective years, Charles at the age of 13, in an act of kindness and love of his family, reluctantly left junior high school to aid in their financial support. He continued to learn the many skills and trades in building, the use of tools and heavy equipment and also found himself performing all sorts of odd jobs to earn the much needed family money. He seemed to take a shine to jobs that involved making things like wire cables, engine blocks, manufacturing, foundry jobs and many hands-on factory type of jobs including running diesel engines to move hot pots of steel into open hearth ovens. He really enjoyed learning about each of these jobs and the hard work itself was just as much fun in his own words.

A first cousin provided him with steady work for a brief period of time prior to joining the Civilian Conservation Corps Camp by cutting, splitting and stacking firewood to sell in the community. Another local resident of the Williamsport area and friend to his mother Laura, took Charles on as her daily errand boy keeping him busy doing all of the things around her house that she was unable to do as a result of her own personal health problems and physical disabilities. Charles always seemed to find a source of work wherever he went and enjoyed it with a great sense of pride ever-knowing that he was truly helping his large and loving family.

Joining the armed forces, going off to war or anything on this scale wasn't a life-long dream of Charles, it just happened to be an opportunity that presented itself at the time. Knowing the great demand for people to take up the fight and the potential for knowledge, travel and a method of providing an income for his family all pointed Charles in the direction of the armed forces, but first some training and time spent in the CCC Camps was in his uncertain future.

A cousin from his mother's side who had previously served in WWI, provided Charles with somewhat of a familiar idea of what it was to be a soldier. Clarence Ardell, who became a victim of mustard gas during this conflict, suffered with what Charles referred to as a *"bad cough"* and a very painful and constant life-long affliction. Another uncle, brother of his father Lyman Libby, also served in the first world war in France. Mr. Libby's memory of his uncle is as such . . .

```
"He never talked much about his time spent
in the army and his fighting during the WWI
conflict. He was kind of a loner and never
really spent too much time with the fam-
ily. He was a very quiet man without much
to say. The only time he really talked about
it was when speaking about the Letter of
Protection which he always carried tucked
away in his pocket."
```

Mr. Libby remembers that the entire family was proud of his Uncle Lyman and Clarence for what they had done and sacrificed while in the war. There was a great amount of pride there and in the back of Charles's young mind, the military option was never ruled out or frowned upon by anyone within his direct family circle. So, as the young Charles made it day by day in the small town he knew as home, his path continued to lead him in many different directions from which he would continue to gain knowledge and above all, common sense. His path, many small jobs and big life lessons, were equally satisfying and fulfilling. They all moved him that much closer to his ultimate assignment of fate which would be far away from the comforts of home, family, friends and the quiet life in Williamsport, Pennsylvania to a war which was happening half way across the world. Leading to a place that he had only dreamed and heard about on the radio and on the movie screen, this strange path would uproot the boy that he was and would ultimately send him home as a man with many memories and lessons to share with his family and the many others who were close to Charles. This path was rough but welcomed by a boy that had fortitude and courage. Qualities that would be necessary for Charles to take care of a military commander while taking orders . . . *"From The Command Car."*

The Civilian Conservation Corps Camps

* * *

IN AN ATTEMPT TO JUMP start and stimulate the US economy and instill the important values of hard work into young American men, President Franklin D. Roosevelt created a process to strengthen and improve our infrastructure as well as providing much needed and important income for their families. Through *The New Deal Program*, the creation of the **Civilian Conservation Corps Camps**, also known as the *CCC Camps*, provided thousands of American family members work and most of all . . . hope!

This program was started in 1933, just thirty seven days after the Roosevelt inauguration and was a brilliant method of uniting skilled and professional civil engineers and the American armed services into one program. The theory was to develop and implement the building of roads, bridges, dikes, dams and many other types of major forestry improvements to help states in the greater Northeastern and Northwestern United States. The first to become employed within the program were unmarried and unemployed men and women between the ages of eighteen and twenty five. The second phase put WWI vets back to work within their own specialized camps. This highly successful program lasted until the year 1942 and was dissolved only for the fact that our great country had rebounded and was starting to prosper financially once again. This uncontroversial program gained wide acceptance and was just one of the many remarkable accomplishments that this sitting president did to help the United States of America and its many hard-working citizens.

CCC Camp Morton workers - Charles Libby - 2nd from right bottom.

Charles Libby was no exception to the rapid enlistment into this enticing and valuable program. Recalling that the first time he ever voted, it was for Roosevelt. Charles highly praises the former president for his insight and desire to truly help the American people of the time. Considering himself a democrat, at that time of the creation of these new programs, Charles believed in the party and saw the many benefits of these working camps. So, at the age of sixteen on April 10, 1934, with pride and excitement, Charles Libby joined the Civilian Conservation Corps Camp S-104-Pa. Near the densely wooded area of Benton, Pennsylvania, Charles was now a working member of **Camp Morton**, just like many of the other promising young men in and around this small town in Pennsylvania.

These camps having both a military and civilian presence appealed to Mr. Libby and he seems to remember that at the time he joined his camp that there were at least five of them across his area of Pennsylvania alone. Eventually, the entire state of Pennsylvania housed one-hundred and thirteen of these hard working and highly beneficial camps. The camp itself was run by US Army military officers with the ranking of either lieutenant or captain. They were there to teach and keep the discipline and help young men to stay on task, help them learn how to take orders and to keep them fit with the necessary drills much like the basic training within the United States Army itself. The camp foreman on each of the job sites was a civilian, most likely an engineer of sorts, and was knowledgeable in that particular task that was asked of the CCC Camp workers with the military officers always keeping a watchful eye on each of the workers. They would all make sure that each of these young boys were holding up their end of the required jobs and important tasks.

CCC Camp officers and foreman. Captain Jack Thompson pictured 3rd from left.

One officer in particular Mr. Libby fondly remembers was Captain Jack Thompson. Walking around the camp sternly and in true military fashion of the day, Captain Jack smoked his cigarette in a long stemmed holder much like that of President Roosevelt. Mr. Libby refers to him as a very good man who ran the CCC Camp without any fooling around. Although each of the members of the CCC Camp wore military-type uniforms and performed each day like our military, they were still to be considered civilian workers. Captain Jack treated them with the respect of a military soldier which was one of his methods of teaching each of them proper discipline, self-respect and preparing them for a life within the military which many of these young men had aimed for from the very start of their service within these camps.

Another figure in charge directly under the command of Captain Jack was Lieutenant Silsbee. Mr. Libby commented that he would take his orders directly from the camp commander Captain Jack and carry them out. Mr. Libby also mentions that even though Silsbee demanded respect from each of the boys and that he too was a very nice guy and treated all of them very well. A third lieutenant that was in charge of the boys was Lt. Evans. Mr. Libby remembers him as also being a nice person and a very good example of a military camp officer.

"As long as you behaved and listened to all of them, they treated you with kindness and respect. You were sent home if you caused any trouble. One boy from the camp said to Captain Jack, as he was loaded into the truck to go home after disobeying orders, that he'd like to punch him in the mouth. Captain Jack said to him that if he wanted to he could get down out of the truck and give it a try. The kid got out of the truck and took a big swing. Captain Jack ducked the punch and knocked him on his butt! Before he got up, he asked him if he'd like to try a second time and he declined. He got back on the truck and headed to the

> railroad station in Harrisburg to go home.
> They gave him a little money for his family
> and sent him on his way."

Fort Hoyle, located in Maryland, was a destination where the boys were taken by train to participate in discipline training and were formerly inducted into the CCC Camps. This exercise was led by the sergeants to see if they were cut out to do the type of work that would be asked of them day in and day out. The boys were placed in a ditch wearing rubber boots and with water half way up their legs and they were told to start shoveling the mud and water out of the trench in the pouring down rain. Mr. Libby recalls that all the boys within his group particular passed the discipline test and were all allowed to stay within the camp and keep their labor job to help their families.

With five barracks in this particular camp that young Charles was stationed in and approximately sixty boys to a barrack, each of these boys would work for a rate of five dollars per month for the young man to keep for his own use and a rate of twenty five dollars per month to be sent back to their family at home. This amount of money that the United States Government paid for participating was certainly a blessing to the many who were accepted within this valuable program.

> "You either worked or you were told to get
> out, pack your bags and go home. They didn't
> fool around when it came to that. This was
> hard work and nobody loafed on the job!"

These barracks became the young boy's new homes. Living there full time and dawning military green fatigues as their type of uniforms, the young men lived a strict lifestyle enjoying it all the while. The other option, starving, seemed like a senseless route to take with their lives. So, the hard work became routine and a blessing to all of those who were fortunate to be a part of a CCC Camp during those tough economic times. Hot of the summer or cold of the winter, the boys all did their assigned jobs with pride and the satisfaction of knowing that their hard work was lifting a great financial burden from their beloved families back home wherever that may have been.

Working out at the CCC Camp, a young and fit Charles Libby gives his best boxing pose.

One luxury the boys had in the camp, which Charles was a part of, was a project that they undertook all on their own. The boys all dug out their own swimming hole to use for the hot summer months. With the aid of a bulldozer and grater, the boys damned up a creek that ran about 100 yards from the camp itself. Using the knowledge that was being taught to them by the civil engineers at the camp, the boys turned that knowledge into a very useful activity for them to take full advantage of. After completion of the large swimming hole, which was the size of a small lake or pond, it took about two or three weeks for the mud and dirt to finally settle and create the ideal conditions for it to be used by all of the boys in the camp. This became a very popular place for the boys each night after their hard work was completed. In the wide open area where the hole was located, the stars and moonlight would provide a well-lit hole for the boys well into the night until the mandatory camp's *lights out* at eleven o'clock. A three-level diving platform was also built and attached to a tree which stood almost ten feet high for the boys to test their diving skills to show off for one-another. A lower grated section gradually led the boys onto shore as a type of in and out of the hole area. A comforting activity for the hard working boys and a visible sign of the skills that they were actively acquiring there each and every day.

Mr. Libby also mentioned that the swimming hole became a place where instructors from the American Red Cross would teach cadets water safety, life-saving, swimming techniques as well as proper resuscitation of a drowning victim. The boys who qualified would receive an arm band to wear whenever they were needed to aid with Red Cross emergencies relating to water rescues in the area of their camp. These were important skills and the boys were glad to help if they were needed for such vital life saving services. Charles, having spent a lot of time swimming in the Susquehanna River near his home, was the perfect candidate for these types of classes.

The swimming hole at Camp Morton built by the CCC boys.

Another service which young Charles was proud to have had a part in was saving the life of a young girl who lived near the CCC Camp. This young girl who lived locally in Benton, PA, had come into her time of maturing as a young lady. The flow of blood was too great from her body and she became very weak and in desperate need for blood to help to save her life. The local hospital desperately needed to find the correct blood type of AB positive to provide her with an urgent transfusion. One of the nurses attending to this young girl recommended to her family that they go to the local CCC Camp to see if there was a qualified donor to help in this serious emergency.

An announcement was made to the boys at the evening meal by Captain Jack Thompson. He told all the boys that there was a girl who was going to die unless someone could step up and help her out by providing blood for the necessary transfusion. After the meal, twenty seven of the boys went to where the medical staff was attending to the girl at her home to see who would be the correct donor type. Upon arrival, all twenty seven of these boys waited outside for their turn to get their blood type matched. While waiting their turn, Mr. Libby remembers that the boys all laid in the grass on this nice day in the month of May. After the completion of the testing, the nurse came outside and announced to all of the boys, "Which one of you boys is Charlie Libby?"

Charles replied that he was that boy and the nurse anxiously told him that they would take him in first. As he walked into the room and saw the girl, Mr. Libby remarked that she already looked as if she was dead from her pale white skin color and the stillness of her ailing and frail body.

Dr. Snyder, who was in charge of her treatment, told young Charles that he would be taking his blood directly from his arm and putting it straight into hers. It had to be done quickly and there was no time for any other known medical methods of transfusions. Mr. Libby remembers this transfusion procedure like it was yesterday and recalls every single detail of this crude but effective procedure . . .

```
"She was actually coming back to life! They
took a pint and three quarters from me be-
cause she really needed it. That's more than
they would usually take from any one per-
son, but I didn't mind if it was going to
help to save her life."
```

After completing the life-saving mission, the doctor told the nurse, "Take this boy down to the kitchen, give him two shots of whiskey first, a quart of milk and a cheese sandwich and make sure he eats it all." Mr. Libby also remembers that they had offered each of the boys twenty five dollars to go and help out. He added more about the money offer during this conversation,

> "At first, I thought it would be a great way
> to send my mother and father an extra $25.
> But afterward, I forgot all about the money
> that they offered me and never asked for it.
> Everybody else forgot about it as well."

Everybody loaded back into the truck and headed back to the camp with a true sense of personal satisfaction knowing that they had all just done something good, especially the young AB positive donor Charlie Libby. Although the other boys on the truck didn't match the ailing girl's blood, they too had the opportunity to donate for others who were in need at the time.

The boys of the camps would be given weekend passes from time to time and Charles was always ready and willing to get back home to see his family. One particular weekend, Charles was headed home, via hitchhiking, and made it there only to be asked to come back due to the health decline once more of this young Seward girl. Captain Jack was urgently alerted by the medical staff that she would need some more of Charlie's blood because it had worked before whereas another boy's blood type had not met her medical needs. The captain asked the others in the camp where they thought Charles would be at that time. They all determined that he would be somewhere at the foot of the North Mountain by then on his return to the camp. Captain Jack himself drove over the mountain in a brand new Hudson to find this much needed blood donor.

Mr. Libby remembers the event as such . . .

> "I remember that he screeched to a halt
> scaring me from the hurried stop. He looked
> at me and asked, "Are you Charlie Libby?"
> I said, yes sir, I am. Captain Jack told me
> that I was going to have to go and give that
> girl another transfusion due to her bleed-
> ing too much once again. He drove me to the

> girl and I was asked to give another full pint of blood. The transfusion helped the young girl almost immediately and I felt good about what I had done for her once again. I could see her color coming back as my blood went into her arm. It was as if all of her energy was back in her body and she actually looked much better."

After the transfusion Charles went into the kitchen of the house. Mr. Seward, the young girl's father, came down to speak with Charles and told him, "Charlie, if I had a million dollars, I would share it with you." He then asked Charles to go back to the girl because she wanted to see him privately before he left to go back to the CCC Camp. With a cracking within his voice Mr. Libby emotionally commented that while she was laying there in the bed he vividly remembers everything about her improved condition.

> "I couldn't believe how much she had improved! She smiled and talked to me, shook my hand as she thanked me for the second blood transfusion. Her color was much better and it seemed that she had some life back in her."

Approximately ten years later, Mr. Libby told me that he contacted her father after finding his telephone number in the phone book. He wanted to see how this girl was doing that he had helped long ago and how everything had turned out with her health. Her father indicated that she had gotten married and that she had three girls of her own. Still appreciative and happy to have heard from Charles, he was still very fond of him and his great gift that he provided to save his precious daughter's life. Mr. Libby still feels that this act of kindness may be one of the reasons that God has given him such a long, healthy, productive and blessed life.

The CCC crew working in a PA winter storm. Charles pictured in back row - 2nd from left.

There are many great memories that still flow through the mind of Mr. Libby about the CCC Camps. Being a hunter, like most young men of Pennsylvania, he fondly remembers that around the camp that the wildlife was abundant and always present. White-tailed deer, wild turkey and the famous Pennsylvania black bear, all made appearances when the boys would be traveling or working near these camps. Mr. Libby also remembers the snow being so high at times that the deer would move out of the wooded areas and stand in the truck tracks on their paths to avoid having to stand in the higher snow drifts. He also remarked that at one time it was so cold that many of the deer had frozen snow attached to the bottoms of their legs and when they ran and made contact with bushes or trees, the crusted snow would get knocked off the legs of the deer also removing their skin, bringing it down to just bare bone in those frozen areas. Needless to say, the boys at the CCC Camps endured some of the very same harsh winter conditions while in the thick woods of Pennsylvania, but always managed to keep their bodies warmer by working hard and keeping some type of physical motion while performing their required chores and camp duties.

The camps provided each of the boys with warm clothing for those freezing days. Not the camouflage that military personnel are provided, but they received felt lines jackets, wool socks and gloves to deal with the frigid weather conditions. Rubber galoshes were worn by each of the boys which kept their feet dry and slightly warmer as they worked in the very deep and wet heavy snow.

During lunch breaks, peanut butter and jelly sandwiches on freshly baked bread from the camp were issued to the boys and the canteens they carried would be filled with hot chocolate during these colder months to keep them as warm as possible. At six o'clock, the boys all knew that supper was going to be ready and waiting for them. Mr. Libby remembers that boiled cabbage, sauerkraut, chipped beef on toast, turkey on Christmas, chicken if turkey was in short supply and other very good food was served to the boys and officers alike. Breakfast offered French toast, freshly gathered scrambled eggs, oatmeal, milk and other foods to give the boys their much needed energy for the hard day's work which they were all about to undertake.

Once while on the road work around the Red Rock area, the boys heard a sharp-pitched whining sound that they couldn't identify. Finally after the third day, they found two baby bear cubs within a stump taking shelter. They rescued these two very small orphaned bear cubs, took them to the mess hall and fabricated two bottles and fed them. This continued for several weeks until the bears got to a decent size. When the camp bugle would sound for any meal and the GI's would assemble in the mess hall, the bear cubs too would assemble out back near the mess hall door to wait for scraps from their newfound parents, the boys and the cooks of the CCC Camp. They became like pet dogs running around the camp and would sometimes frighten unknowing visitors that were coming to see their sons at the camp on Sunday's during visiting hours. On the colder nights, the bears could even be found sleeping under one of the boy's cot as if they belonged there and were part of the crew. The bears must had provided a sense of home as if they had their pets there with them to take away a little of the loneliness that these young boys must had all felt being away from home for many for the first time ever.

One day, the game warden in the area came into the camp and took the bears to find them a more suitable home in the woods away from the camp. Mr. Libby remembered that none of the boys at the CCC Camp were too happy when they took these bears that had become just like a part of their family. But, there was nothing they could do about it and life at the camp went on as usual without their two loveable black bear friends. Mr. Libby remarked about the day their took them away . . .

> "None of us were too happy about it. They had become like a pet dog to us and we really loved them. But, there was nothing that any of us could do and we had to let them go with the warden."

Charles had many jobs that he was introduced to while at this camp which were both challenging as well as what he referred to as "back breaking". A spot on the dynamite crew placed Charles with an eight pound sledge hammer in his hands swinging it all day long alternating with the star bit making the necessary hole that was needed for the blasting. This was a technique to take out tree stumps and large boulders that would become fire trails and eventually the major highways which now run throughout the state of Pennsylvania. Bridges, dams and other types of necessary structures were also built due to the hard work of these tough young men. In a special way, they are the unsung heroes of our early Pennsylvania history and these boys deserve a big salute for their very important and unselfish contributions.

Breaking rocks along the pathways and working hard throughout the day was all part of the normal routine for these young men. Mr. Libby remembers watching his foreman setting the dynamite and the nitroglycerine before placing the blasting caps that would start the charge for the pending explosion. He said that it looked very dangerous and they always took their time and great care when doing this aspect of their job. Mr. Libby smiles as he tells a humorous story about the time that he had to relieve himself in the woods just prior to one of these powerful explosions. . .

```
"I had to go really bad! I had gone into
the woods not too far away from where we
were working, not knowing how soon the next
blast would be. I heard the words being
yelled FIRE in the hole! And I knew that
it was about to happen. I was mid-stream
and couldn't stop myself. I stood there and
heard the loud BANG! The next thing I knew,
a big rock landed just inches in front of me
crashing to the ground. It sure scared me
and after that, I was sure to relieve myself
in a safer place out of range."
```

A camp foreman named Lou Dudder, once approached Charles and offered him the job of taking care of the foreman's quarters as an orderly to which Charles proudly agreed. His duties would entail making beds, keeping the fireplace clean and straightening up the officer's quarters when needed. This also meant that his laboring on the dynamite crew was limited to only when they needed extra hands on a big job. That was something that also appealed to Charles, especially in the cold of winter and heat of the summer months.

Charles was also able to make a little extra money from the officers and men that would travel into town on the weekends by pressing their pants for twenty five cents a pair to prepare for the dances held at their recreation hall near their camp. In addition to these dances, friday nights at West Side Park in Berwick, PA was the popular destination for the local nurses from the Bloomsburg Hospital to dance with these boys. A physical education teacher placed an ad in the local paper advertising for young women to come and dance with the boys of the CCC Camps. This turned out to be very successful with an entire truckload of women showing up as well as the six or eight thrown in the captain's car to dance with these hard working boys.

For $1.65, the boys would attend concerts which featured many big bands of the area. Some of the performers that Mr. Libby remembers include Chick Webb, Mal Hallett, Wayne King, the now famous Guy Lombardo and many others who would come to perform about every three months.

```
"I had good times while I was in there. I
really love to dance and especially loved
the type of music that they played for us!
I got to see many of the greats back in the
day."
```

Mr. Libby remembers that they took very good care of all of them providing all their basic necessities, medical care and attempted to give them some of the comforts of home. In answering questions about the interaction with the other boys, Mr. Libby remembers an unfortunate incident which happened one particular day in the mess hall.

```
"The meals were good and we had everything
we needed. I remember an apple fight in the
chow house one day which got me into some
trouble. I tossed one back at the crowd that
was thrown at me after I got hit. I guess
I was so mad that I threw it a little hard
and knocked another boy right out. I wasn't
```

```
sure if it was mine that hit him, but I felt
really bad about it."
```

Mr. Libby remembers Captain Jack asking the entire group about who threw the apple that caused the young boy to be knocked out and expressed that there would be no more fresh fruit in the chow house for the boys until someone told him who threw it. Later that night, young Charles went to Captain Jack's barracks and told him that it may have been him that did it and that he was very sorry that it happened. Captain Jack told him that he was proud of him for his honesty and courage and dismissed him from any trouble. Later at the meal, Captain Jack announced to the entire camp that the matter with the flying fruit had been taken care of and that the subject was now closed. No more was ever mentioned about it and Charles felt a little more mature for how he had handled the entire situation with honesty and integrity.

Until the destructive flooding of 1936 in Pennsylvania, Charles enjoyed his time in the CCC Camps calling these some of the best times of his life. Always helping his family in one form or another, Charles was asked by his pleading father to come home after the flood waters had receded to help in the efforts of cleaning up the deep mud and debris that filled the bottom portions of the house after the eight foot of rushing water overtook these lower levels of their family's home.

Charles had to report to Captain Jack and put in the formal request to leave the camp. He recalls the words of his superior telling him that he was a fine boy and he'd personally do the paperwork so that he could get home right away and that he'd also personally take him into Bloomsburg, PA so that he could catch the bus home. He also recalls asking the captain to leave was with deep regret and much sadness. He starts to cry as he tells the moment that he had to ask to go home to help his father with the clean up. . .

```
"I told him that I really don't want to leave
Captain. I like it here very much but my dad
really needs my help at home."
```

After the car ride to the bus stop, it was the last time that Charles ever saw Captain Jack. He still remembers him fondly with a great amount of respect and admiration for this strict but compassionate man of the CCC Camp whom he worked for. And so it was that on March 31, 1936, young Charles Libby was "Honorably Discharged" from the Civilian Conservation Corps.

Charles didn't return to the camps after his leaving due to the great amount of work that needed to be done at his family's home with such chores as hosing and shoveling mud and debris as well as the many repairs that needed to be done from the massive destruction which this flood had caused to his family's home. For a short time, Charles also helped out financially as he found work on a garbage route near his home as a laborer with a man named Kenny Webb. At this point, Charles got his first driver's license and was ready to drive, perform labor work or do whatever he needed to do to stay employed and help out as needed.

After his daily work was done, Mr. Libby remembers coming home and hearing reports on the radio about Adolf Hitler and the countries he invaded like Poland and others on his evil rampage. Mr. Libby recalls one thought from these early reports they heard. . .

```
"I thought to myself, someday he is going
to try to come and get us here in the US.
I knew that someone had to stop this guy,
and FAST!"
```

Mr. Libby feels that the CCC Camps were a starting point and influence to him as for his choice to join the United States military. After all, they were basically military camps and he found that he liked it very much and did extremely well with the disciplined lifestyle. I asked Mr. Libby if he thought the CCC Camps would work and help us once again today and Mr. Libby replied to the question with a quick and stern response . . .

"No! Kids today are too damn lazy and care more about dope. We never had dope around us and we worked hard. They are beyond help today. Back then we didn't talk about it or take any interest in it. The kids today wouldn't be able to cope with the discipline that is involved in a camp of this type. They wouldn't want to put their own lives on hold to work that hard and listen to an authority figure. The good ones now already enlist in the armed services and the others just couldn't handle the camps at all! They would be a good thing, but I don't believe that they would have anyone sign up for them like we did."

Strong words of frustration, sadness and disappointment from a man that has seen the cultural changes of our generations and a decline in work ethics and for what seems to be important to youth today. That's the way he sees it and looking through the eyes of a man that has seen hard working soldiers go into battle, some surviving and some dying, I could hear the many emotions and disappointment within his voice as he states this strong belief. It is sad that a war hero has to feel this way and especially sad that there is more than just a fraction of truth within what he says and feels. God bless and save our great nation from the lack of integrity and lack of hard work that each and every American should perform and contribute to our society each and every day!

SO, this brings an end to the days of Charles Libby serving and working in Camp Morton, a CCC Camp in Benton, Pennsylvania. NOW . . . fast-foward 80 years! Lets add a new twist on this old story and tug at the heart strings of anyone who has ever helped another human being and felt a sense of accomplishment. This new story brings forth another interesting compliment to the story of the blood transfusion that occurred while working in the CCC Camp.

As an interviewer of Mr. Libby, I have to tell readers that when you speak to Mr. Libby and ask him to tell you a story, he most often goes to the CCC Camp blood transfusion experience first! This great feeling of satisfaction has always been a high-point of his younger life prior to his service in WWII but not without the lifelong need for some sense of closure. He often said to me in conversations . . .

```
"I wonder what ever happened to that young
girl that I gave the transfusion to?"
```

As he relives that memory of seeing her in a sense of coming back to life, his voice cracks ever so slightly and you can feel the emotions in the room as he relives that exact moment over eighty years ago.

On May 11, 2015, Mr. Libby and myself were asked to give a speech at a restaurant in Benton, PA near the site of the former CCC Camp that he was based out of during his teen years. The Brass Pelican was the meeting place for over 90 people that were enthralled with his stories of these camps. Many had an intense interest in these stories as they eagerly waited to possibly hear the names of their own relatives who also worked within this camp of young boys. Mr. Libby himself was full of excitement and enthusiasm as he mentally prepared himself to give a speech full of his stories and experiences of his younger days.

As the people were entering the restaurant, Mr. Libby would glance to the door to smile and wave to all of the people that came to listen and enjoy a glimpse into their town's rich history. I could sense a hope within Mr. Libby that someone would walk through the door from either the camp itself or from his past as a type of reunion. He often mentions within our long talks how he was a blessed man to live as long as he has but closes each memory with the remark . . .

```
"They're probably all gone now. I've out-
lived all my family and most of my friends.
I'm pretty sure that I am one of the last
ones still living."
```

As I watched the many people entering and the room filling up to it's capacity, conversation grew between the guests as they shared their own stories, hopes and desires for some sense of information to complete an old family story as well as the brief exchanges of old family photos, news clippings and small pieces of memoribilia from the camp itself. I had noticed three women entering the restaurant with a sense of urgency as well as a determined purpose to sit as close to Mr. Libby as possible. Moving their way to the very front of the room at a table near us, they sat their personals on the table and wasted no time to approach Mr. Libby to introduce themselves.

"*Charlie Libby?*" the first woman asked as she extended her hand out to him. "*Why yes!*" he answered with a big smile and warm handshake. The woman then responded to Mr. Libby with some of the most heart-warming words that I have ever heard in my life as she cupped the hands of a man that has worked hard his entire life. With a look of deep admiration and warmth, she looked into his eyes and spoke to him.

```
"We have heard about you for our entire
lives. We have always wanted to meet you
and to tell you how much we appreciate what
you did for our mother when she was a young
girl."
```

The second woman joined her and also took his hands as they explained to Mr. Libby just who they were. With a smile from his face and a deep breath which seemed to me much like a sense of closure that he had searched for these many years, the women identified themselves as two of the daughters of the young girl that young Charles had given the transfusion to almost 80 years ago! By now, the three of them were all huddled into a tight circle just looking at one-another in a frozen moment in time that was as special for them as words can not describe. The many emotions of love, happiness, gratitude as well as that sense of closure filled the room much like the Holy Spirit when he enters you in your time of great need. As he turned and looked at me with his eyes welling up, he smiled and asked me if I knew who they were. I had been the *fly on the wall* during this entire event and indicated that I knew exactly who they were. I myself moved into the energy of the moment and shook their hands and told them how wonderful it was to meet the both of them. Then, the line that did it for Mr. Libby was spoken by one of the sisters that brought his unselfish deed to an entirely new light for Mr. Libby and his blessed life seemed even more important at that exact moment . . . *"You know, we have your blood running through our veins. We owe you so much and we think that you are an angel."*

Mr. Charles Libby (age 97) pictured with the daughters of Irene Seward. Left – Patsy Truskoloski, Right – Glenda Lechleitner

Then, in true Mr. Libby fashion, he began to tell the two his story about their own mother without waiting for the presentation to begin. I usually scold him when we do these types of events and joke to him by saying, "You're going to give away all our good stories before the speech even starts!" But at this occasion, I felt it better for him to talk away and allow him the opportunity to speak to these women about their mother and finally hear it from the man that saved her life all those many years ago.

The entire event after this meeting was magical for all of us who had just experienced that beautiful moment. I caught Mr. Libby looking their way many times throughout his entire presentation as if he was trying his best to look at each of these women to see a glimpse of their mother in their own features. The entire event went very well and we later met the two back at the Brass Pelican to enjoy a breakfast of buckwheat pancakes, liverwurst, scrapple and other Pennsylvania favorites. Photos filled the table, stories filled the air and smiles filled all of our faces throughout the entire meal. I was able to find out through some questioning some of the details of the past years that helped Mr. Libby fill in the blanks of his thoughts for those many unknowns.

A quick travel through time to give a few of those details to make the story complete. . .

Mr. Libby found it satisfying to know that the young girl, Irene Seward, had married and became the mother of three healthy girls. Patsy and Glenda are the two daughters that were present at the restaurant for this historic speech and a third middle sister named Karla. The young Seward girl had become the wife of Leo Lechleitner and they were happily married for over fifty years! She has since passed away in 2004 but not without telling her story often to her daughters about the young Charles Libby. The family had also learned years ago that the urgent need for their mother's transfusion was contributed to two seperate childhood diseases that she had contracted at once. This was something that also wasn't known at the time that Charles had been asked to help her. Special thanks to the daughters of Irene, Patsy and Glenda, for their contribution and memories shared with this great man who has been blessed once again by knowing how things went in the life of that young girl that he so fondly remembers.

The day of the speech was not to end with just the goodbyes of the guests and the last minute hand shakes and autographs that Mr. Libby had to sign. There was one more treat for him to experience with the help of a local PA Game Commission Officer named William Williams, who is the Information and Education Supervisor for the PA Game Commission, NE Region. Bill invited us both to take a ride with him to the actual site of the former Camp Morton. This would mark the first time that Mr. Libby had visited the camp site since he left to go home as a teen.

Author Steve Hunter and Mr. Libby at the former
site of Camp Morton in Benton, PA.

Mr. Libby didn't know what to think and certainly didn't know what to expect to see with so much time passing by since the days of operation in this CCC Camp. We arrived at the site to see a very nice hand-carved sign that marks the actual entrance and acts as a type of official marker of it's rich history. We couldn't resist standing next to the sign for a quick photo and the others who had followed us there also took their share of photos with Mr. Libby beside the newly placed sign. Beaming with pride, Mr. Libby smiled for these photos and seemed to be transported back in time as he felt the energy of the site that he not only lived for a time as a youth, but a wonderful place that helped to shape him as a man.

Bill explained that where we were would have been the road that took you to the main entrance of the camp as we walked several yards to a grassy field to our left that would have marked the area of the main camp gate as well as many of the buildings that became their actual barracks. As Mr. Libby looked over the large field, you could see that he actually saw the former buildings where they had stood those many years ago. You could also tell that he was flooded with fond memories of this place itself. As we walked along the road, you could still see many of the large stones that were placed there by the boys to line the path in a short wall-type formation. A true testement that what the boys had built with their own hands, still remained. The path was also lined with very large Hemlock trees that stood as much as 100 feet tall. Bill asked Mr. Libby if he remembered any of these trees and Mr. Libby proudly spoke to the group once again telling his version of the story. . .

```
"There were no trees here when I was in the
camp. We held the sprigs in the palm of our
hands and walked the path planting each and
every one of the trees that see here now.
They were just tiny little branches and now
look at them! You can't even get your arms
around these giants!"
```

We wasted no time to get Mr. Libby standing by one of these magestic trees for some more photos. Not very often that anyone can get a photo of a tree so big with one of the planters admiring it at this stage of growth. While looking between these trees and past the grass field, you could see the mountain that many of the boys found as a challenge to climb in their free time to test their climbing skills and to catch a view of the camp from the top of this rocky outpost. Being a hunter and avid outdoorsman, I myself was in awe of the height, the rugged terrain and the steep angle of this mountain that the boys had challeneged many times while at this camp. A photo that Mr. Libby took with his own camera as a teen looks down at the camp itself making the barracks look like just small cabins. I asked Mr. Libby about the climb while we stood there and looked at this marvelous piece of the mountain and he replied . . .

```
"I was very fit back then and it was still
hard for me to climb it. But, I did it pretty
quickly and enjoyed getting up to the top
and looking down at the camp. Many of us
would do it and just relax up there. We all
really enjoyed the climb and the view as
well."
```

A view of Camp Morton from the nearby mountain top.

We all continued down the path slowly to allow Mr. Libby to keep up with all of us as well as not to miss any of the stories that he may have for us as we moved toward another of the fond memories for Mr. Libby, the famous swimming hole. This swimming hole was also talked about by many of the people that attended the speech this day. It seems that many of the boys that lived in the area of the camp prior to serving, came home before going off to war with stories of this fun place and the big accomplishment for them to had built it.

We got to the end of the road and Bill explained along with one other gentleman and woman that were there, just where the hole would have been. We also had to understand that between now and that time, there were several floods that all changed the landscape and made it fairly unrecognizeable for us to see and compare to the photos. We also tried to place exactly where the diving platform may had been and Mr. Libby was quick to point in a general direction and clear it up for all of us. I took it upon myself to drop down over the bank to explore a little to see if I could find any type of pattern or anything that resembled the work that had been done to the area for such a project. After close examination, we were all able to find an outline of where the boys had damned up the water, a place that still had some rock work that may have been a shoring up of a wall and a small grade where the entrance of the hole may have been positioned.

To all of us, that was a successful investigation and to Mr. Libby, the fact that he was standing anywhere close to this sacred spot was good enough for him. I fancy myself as a rock collector and enjoy having one from any place that I visit that has some special meaning to me. I wasted no time in choosing one that would fit into my pocket from the area as a souvenir for my collection and possibly one that was touched by these boys back in a time that they served our great country doing what they did. I also picked one for Mr. Libby and at the end of the day, gave it to him and said that he may have touched this 80 years ago while in that swimming hole. He looked at it and put it into his shirt pocket. I am not sure what he did with it, but I am sure that it probably went into his personal collection of things that mean so much to him from his time spent in the CCC Camp.

We all moved back to the vehicles and headed back home with new memories that Mr. Libby and I could now share together. Bill Williams has written an article that will appear in an upcoming edition of The PA Game News and for Mr. Libby, he fills in just one more empty space to see what has become of Camp Morton. On the drive home, Mr. Libby spoke privately to me about the day as such . . .

> "Today was a great day! I am so happy that so many people came out to see me and hear my stories. I can't believe that so many people were interested in the CCC Camp there. I never knew how important of a job we did until they all asked me so many questions, shook my hand and thanked me for what I did. It was a great day!"

CCC Camps showed true American spirit and their ability to work hard and meet our challenges head-on with fortitude and success. Their contributions to this great country are not as well-known as many other events in our history, but were just as important. These great men deserve our sincere thanks and gratitude. Hopefully, their memory will be kept alive through these facts and stories within this manuscript. To all who participated "THANK YOU!"

Enlistment, Basics and My Unit

✳ ✳ ✳

A TIME OF NEED WAS fed by a time of great sacrifice. Seeds planted in an empty field of desperation turning out a crop of young *boys* that became *men* faster than life itself could had provided under normal circumstances. The romanticism of going off to war and the duty sworn to their country was far more involved than just dawning the uniform of an American soldier. Sacrificing oneself for saving the world provided film-makers with plenty of material to use in John Wayne movies, but never came near the sights, smells and sounds that each of these young men would encounter as they literally drove, marched, flew, fought and sometimes crawled across the entire war-torn and bloody continent of Europe.

Enlistment into the armed services and avoiding the unknowns of the draft provided an opportunity for these young men to at least attempt some form of a choice and area of expertise as to what they would be asked to do or perform when finally called up for duty. Airmen, tank drivers, naval ship crewman, medical corp., mechanics, officers for the educated ones, drivers or just plain old grunts, all found their own nitch in serving. The lists were long and the men knew that they needed to be filled if we as a country were going to be successful. Boys and men of all ages proudly enlisted into service. Charles A. Libby reported to armory building on Pine Street in Williamsport, PA, walked through the door and proudly enlisted in The PA National Guard. This particular building and branch of service was close to the home of Charles Libby and provided an easy and convenient opportunity to get started in his military service after being convinced by a neighborhood friend, Ernest Kirschbaum, to do so. The sense of pride and the following in his two uncle's footsteps seemed to be the proper and honorable thing for Charles to do.

Officially, Charles enlisted on February 3rd of 1941 and was inducted into active service on February 17th. Now Private Charles A. Libby of The National Guard 109th Infantry Unit, was ready to learn all new routines that would be asked of him from the guard. Close-order drills, marching techniques, and much more were all included in his new training, certainly an activity that was helped by his time within the CCC Camp. Seeing things in a different light and becoming wiser through a forced understanding of the difference between life and death was something that these young men and women would soon acquire. A shot in both arms, which would protect them from tetanus and typhoid, but neither of these shots would protect from the horrors that they would see day after day and the feelings of sadness, loneliness and the fear of death within their inner-self.

Regular Army now, Charles Libby dressed in his uniform.

Three weeks of the required six recruits would normally spend near their hometown learning the special skills of the National Guard was all they had time for as the unit was ordered into regular federal service due to the increase of troop movement in Europe. At this point, the 109th Infantry Unit of The Pennsylvania National Guard became what Mr. Libby referred to as *regular army*. Quite a journey from a young boy jumping on trains, to the CCC Camps, to the Pennsylvania National Guard and now a member of The United States Army. Charles Libby's life in his younger years was full of excitement and plenty of personal satisfaction which laid down a solid foundation for years of experience for which was to certainly follow.

Indiantown Gap, PA provided the men of this unit with a new home away from home. An encampment nestled in the mountains of Lebanon and Dauphin County, Fort Indiantown Gap is located twenty three miles northeast of Pennsylvania's capital city of Harrisburg. This would be the base of operations for these boys from the Williamsport unit. Between their rigorous schedule of maneuvers, which they were about to undertake to prepare for warfare on a completely different continent, to this point of intense training which would be of greater importance. It also started a period of time and countdown before shipping to Europe for the young men of this fresh new unit.

Combat training, concealment, camouflaging, map and compass reading, driving all military vehicles and basic machine and weapons operations would provide the troops with the necessary skill sets that they would need for their particular job as well as survival itself in the unfamiliar and rough terrain of the European continent. Preparedness and mock battles as a sort of *war games*, would be staged for various situations but still nothing could prepare them for the many horrors of combat that would befall them soon in their very young lives.

Preparedness was first and foremost for each branch of our military and prior to these young boys crossing an ocean that once only meant to them a place to vacation, these games and mock battles gave these new soldiers a look at different terrains to better prepare them for their possible locations within the European Theater of operations.

> "One of the first things we had to do was to go into a building that they had set up and walk its entire length without a gas mask while they filled it with three different kinds of smoke including small levels of mustard gas. The barn-type of building was really long and it took a while to get through it. They made us walk and we weren't allowed to run through it or we would have to walk it again. It burned your eyes and your throat really bad! Some of the guys in my unit were throwing up afterward but we all still had to do it at least one time. They used gas in WWI and they knew that we may have to deal with it like they did so they wanted us to know what it was like. None of us liked it at all!"

The marksmanship award was achieved by shooting a series of five shots on the range which measured two-hundred yards. Several recruits lined up and had spotters who would verify the accuracy of your shots fired down range.

> "I qualified for this one without any problems. I paid attention and was very familiar with guns from my hunting experience there in the woods of Pennsylvania."

Young Charles Libby had always taken pride in himself and the perception of how others saw him. He felt that if he was a soldier in the United States Army, he was going to look like a proud soldier. He took great care to always have his uniform pressed and required everything to be worn neatly and in its proper place. One particular memory of this time reflects that when company commander Captain Lentz called him forward in front of all the other soldiers and the newer recruits.

"Captain Lentz said to me, Private Libby, front and center. I walked up looking neat and looking like a soldier. I was up there all alone in front of the whole bunch and beginning to feel a little uncomfortable. Captain Lentz said to everyone, Look at this boy! He's only been here two weeks and looks more like a soldier than all of you. I expect you non-coms to look more like this soldier here. I felt like melting at that moment, but knew that I was acting and looking like a good soldier which made me very proud."

Tent City where Charles Libby signed up for transfer into the new tank outfit.

One day while walking down the street in Fort Indiantown Gap, young Charles ran into his good friend Ernest Kirschbaum from Williamsport who was now in the 109th Field Artillery. Not too happy with some of the guys in the unit at the time, Charles wondered if he could get out of his current unit and into the same one as his friend. He told Charles that on Sunday's you could go over to what they referred to as *Tent City* and sign up for the anti-tank outfit that they were just starting there. This would become the first field artillery combat unit for the United States Army. So, he did just that! He walked into Tent City on the very next Sunday and was anxiously greeted by the men there who asked him, "Would you like to join us?" They also asked him if he had any friends that he wanted to sign up as well. Charles signed up not only himself, but some of his friends that he knew wanted out of their current unit. Charles then went back to the camp and told one of the soldiers in particular that he was having the personal trouble with, that he was getting out of the unit. That same week, Sgt. Getchin came to the men while working on a map problem and announced, "Libby, Bik, Phillips, Peterson" and four other names which escape Mr. Libby, "you guys turn your bedding into the supply tent and report down to Tent City right away!" So each of them followed the order and reported there happily. Mr. Libby said that the unit was already established in their respective tents and assigned each of them to their own division of either A-Company, B-Company, C-Company or the Reconnaissance Unit.

```
"We were all divided up and I was to imme-
diately report to C-Company. I really didn't
care which unit they placed me in, I was
just glad to be out of my old outfit and
into this new one that was just forming.
The boys that I had signed up that day all
thanked me later on about signing them up. I
was a little worried that they would be mad
at me for doing it without them knowing, but
they all said that they were happier in this
new unit and out of the infantry."
```

Charles was later given special permission to visit his old outfit where he was able to tell them all about his new position which was given to him of driving a jeep for an officer within this newly formed unit. Other soldiers asked repeatedly how they could get down there to Tent City and join in with this unit. But, Charles would not divulge the information so that he wouldn't flood them with too many requests and possibly jeopardize his newfound position that he loved so much. He felt proud and very privileged that he would have such a job as taking care of the men who would ultimately be responsible for so many of our soldiers when they reached the battlefields of Europe. This type of job was not only important but one that required a quick thinker, a talented driver and a man that could perform his duty well under the most extreme of any type of conditions.

Mock battles in Fredericksburg, Virginia, Louisiana and Tennessee in the swamps, woods, mountains and various geographical landforms and terrains would better acquaint the boys with what they may encounter in Europe. No formal classroom training for these boys, just reporting to the area outside where they would be trained in the use of the proper military gear or land maps for the day and their specialized training began. There was nothing but real life, hands-on training for these boys. There was no fluff, classroom theory or pretending, they had to know how to use these important tools or they would someday get lost, captured or shot dead according to Mr. Libby.

This advanced training and the various maneuvers began with a short trip from Pennsylvania to AP Hill, Virginia. This fort provided training to the men in the areas of snow and extreme cold weather survival. The boys had to learn to cope with the bad weather in four foot deep snow. All of the fresh soldiers were required to master the techniques of keeping warm which included the actual building of huts and shelters to stay warm. These make-shift huts, of sorts, were erected quickly from scraps provided from a local lumber mill. With hammers and nails which the local community hardware store had donated, the boys made use of whatever was available to them to keep out of the cold wind and hard blowing snow.

> "You had to learn quickly how to build a version of a home to survive the cold weather. We would also get hay from a local barn to line the hut to stay even warmer. We were there about six weeks living like that each and every cold day and each and every colder night."

The use of snow to pile up against the building was a valuable form of concealment as part of their training. The men were told of the snow and eventual weather they would encounter when they reached Europe. Each morning the men were required to assemble for roll call. This was in part to being an army company and also making sure that a member of this unit hadn't frozen to death in the middle of the night.

> "You weren't permitted to start a fire in your hut. You just had to endure it. Some of the guys went to the hardware store and bought oil heaters to keep in their huts and they always stunk of oil fuel. We toughed it out, the four of us in our hut. No oil heat for us. Bik, Peterson, Phillips and I were all crammed in the small living quarters that we built with our own hands."

Valuable training, valuable lessons learned and just the first step to gaining the necessary knowledge that was needed for their trip across the ocean to meet the enemy head-on! The huts were all left standing, personal gear packed up, hammers and saws returned to the hardware store and this fresh unit of recruits were off to return for a short stay to their home base in Fort Indiantown Gap, PA.

A location in Wadesboro, North Carolina was the next stop for the fresh anti-tank unit. Driving to this location in their half-tracks, jeeps, weapons carriers, personal carriers and some motorcycle police escorts, the men drove straight through cities and countryside alike. There was no stopping for traffic lights for these tank GI's. With plenty of onlookers on the roadside, the boys made their way to their next location just like they would be doing when they reached cities in France, Belgium and Germany. A small city of canvas pup tents at night as their BIVOUAC, a temporary encampment on an old logging road in the bad weather or just a blanket pulled up over their heads on the ground would be there home for the night as they moved toward there next camp location for some more vital specialized military and survival training.

This aspect of training for the unit in North Carolina consisted of some of the most important that they would have to master. During this particular assignment, the men would have to become more familiar with the specialized training that they would be asked to perform when arriving to the actual battlefield so tanks and mechanized training became their new daily routine and lifestyle.

> "You had to know how to check everything on the vehicle that you drove. It became just like your very own baby. You had look into everything and know how to maintain it and fix it if needed. It was up to you and nobody else to have this important knowledge."

M-10 tanks, half-tracks and every type of vehicle that would be a part of the 628th when arriving in Europe were massed here in North Carolina and put to the test by its new operators. This was the testing ground and the place where you either learned it and mastered it or you would certainly be in trouble when you reached foreign soil. Another certain fate would be that if you didn't learn it, you'd end up back in the infantry unit with an entirely new job on the many dangerous front lines.

"We had the M-10 tanks over here on maneuvers. This was a diesel powered tank which was miserable to drive. The fumes were unbearable at times while driving them or if you got stuck behind one of these tanks. We were all glad that we had another type of tank when we finally got to England. They served as a practice tank to learn how to handle one but nobody in the unit really liked them."

Trainers from within the army would properly set up an obstacle course which each of the men from this unit would have to successfully complete. A series of rolled barbed wire to crawl under with live gun fire over their heads was just one of the dangerous challenges of this particular army training course. With this razor-sharp wire only four feet off the ground, the soldiers had to stay very low and keep their backs and heads down or they would most certainly stand the chance of getting killed in this dangerous training session before ever reaching the actual battles they were training for.

"They actually had live ammunition in this exercise! One of the guys I knew from Williamsport got hit by a ricochet and it hit him in right the stomach. It spun around and never hit anything too serious, but he didn't have to go to Europe and was sent home. The tripod had loosened up and lowered the line of fire over the course. The live round hit a nearby tree and that's the one that got him. An officer noticed what had happened to the gun and adjusted it right away so that the others could finish their required course. Another guy got so scared

```
on the course that he froze and was crying
like a baby. They had to stop the program
and physically get him out of there. After
they got him out, we resumed the course and
got back to business. I guess the live fire
over his head really got to him. I heard
that they put him in another outfit after
that."
```

The next day, after a rain storm, they had to go through the course once again. Ordered to do it without rain jackets, the men performed it once again for the high-ranking officers who were present that particular day. With a few men not too happy about the conditions of the course, they did it anyway and completed it quickly and properly to impress these key officers. Covered in mud from the course, the men showed their ability to handle this type of situation with prowess and with great speed according to Mr. Libby.

Other tasks in North Carolina included some basic hand-to-hand self-defense training which included disarming the enemy by tripping or sweeping the leg and stabbing them in the vital area within the mid-section. All skills that may be necessary when reaching the battlefield against an enemy that was there waiting to kill anyone that wore a uniform other than the ones provided by the German army under its military commander, Adolf Hitler.

The 40MM cannon fired a shell that stood almost three feet high. The training of this anti-tank gun was done with the use of a tripod on wheels and placed high demands on its operators. The location that the shell would end up was the key to the mastering of its operations. Lobbing a shell to a target was something of a task to determine the distance and the height that you fired it and required equations that needed to be figured out quickly and accurately.

```
"We didn't have that type of weapon for very
long and I was kind of glad when we got rid
```

```
of that particular piece of equipment. It
was really hard to maneuver and even harder
to learn how to operate."
```

This was just another weapon in the arsenal of the 628th that would undergo the necessary improvements, alterations and upgrades along the way. New weapons would be introduced to the men of the 628th as they reached the base in England, especially the newer tank model that was a big improvement on the type of warfare that they would be known for during WWII.

Once again, the men made the long drive back to Fort Indiantown Gap, PA to regroup and get some well-deserved rest. After three months of intense training, it was time to digest this vital information and prepare for the next round that was about to challenge them. All-the-while, the Germans had escalated their attacks on their neighbors and was becoming a stronger force to deal with. Time was ticking away and many people were dying. The 628th was also becoming mightier and more prepared each and every day as they trained it's men to be an intricate part of the eminent defeat of the German armies.

Camp Livingston, Louisiana would prove to be the next important stop for these men of the anti-tank unit, which would change their entire identity and duties when arriving in Europe. Upon arrival to this camp, the men were gathered in the mess hall and told by their superior officers that they would be learning more about the operations of the M-10 Tank and that they would no longer be considered an anti-tank unit. The new title that this unit would receive would be *tank destroyers*. This meant that they would have a more involved job that would place them in the thickest of the battles and that they would be led by a general that would become one of the greatest and well-known in our proud US military history, General George S. Patton.

Louisiana had a terrain that provided the new tank destroyer unit with many new and unique challenges. The M-10 tanks were in place here at Camp Livingston which was a large US Army base. The men were taken there for one purpose and one purpose only, to learn and master the proper operations, mechanics and the ability to drive a tank. Tank driving instructors were in the service long before the fresh recruits of this newly formed tank destroyer unit and made great teachers for this new unit. A driver's license was the first requirement to be chosen for this job. Young Charles had already been driving a weapons carrier and was being trained on these duties which precluded him from the larger tank that the unit was driving.

> "I found it interesting to watch the guys learning how to drive them. I didn't have much time to talk to them about it, but I knew that it was very important stuff that they were doing. I had my own job that I was learning how to do."

This camp proved to be an important change for the young Charles Libby which would affect his duties as a soldier here in the US as well as when he would ultimately deploy to Europe. Charles was already an officer's orderly and had several duties that aided in the everyday activities of the officers within his unit. At this point of his service within his unit, about a year had already passed and his commitment to duty and his integrity had been established with the higher ranking officers. Sergeant Luckey called Charles to his tent one evening and asked if he would like to replace the personal driver for Captain Gallagher. His current driver was going home after turning the age of thirty eight. At that point in time at that age, they were out of the outfit. Little did they know that only two months later, after increased escalation of the war in Europe, they would all be called back to active duty regardless of their age. But, Charles now had the job and remembers the day very well that he was asked to take on this particular new duty. . .

> "He asked me if I wanted the job as Captain Gallagher's driver. He already liked me and knew how I dressed and how I conducted

> myself as well as acting like a gentleman. At first I told him that I didn't want that *dog robber* job. He said to me, Libby you don't have to do KP, long hikes, extra duty or guard duty. I asked him, *when can I start?* I'm glad that I took the job. I stood out and felt kind of important now that I got to drive a Command Car."

Charles immediately reported to the officer's quarters to get his new assignment and an orderly from another company gave him the inside scoop of how to properly tend to these officers as well as how to get along with them. The next step was to report to Captain William Gallagher, commander of C-Company himself.

> "I remember that he said, well Libby, I'm glad you took the job and I think you'll do fine. He told me that there would be some little details that I may need you to do but that will come in time."

Later, the captain asked Charles if he liked the job and the errands that he would send him on. He told him that he really enjoyed the fact that he had a little more freedom at that point to travel and perform these types of duties for him. With a big smile, Mr. Libby spoke about how important he felt to have the job of a Command Car driver. . .

> "We stood out when asked to do these jobs, all of us drivers. I did my job like a soldier and enjoyed all of it. Sometimes he sent me into town and told me not to come back until supper time. I'd go to a local

> diner or bar and have a bite to eat and a few beers and answer questions from the local girls that were impressed by my uniform. I kinda liked that part of my job."

The Command Car itself was a unique newer piece of equipment which the US Army had for their high officers. This vehicle was tan in color and designed without doors and a removable canvas covering on each side. Each covering had a plastic-type window that was open at all times. There were two separated seats in the front of the vehicle and one long waterproof, padded seat which could seat three officers in the back. Mr. Libby also recalls that the seats of the vehicle were very comfortable for the officers. This standard shift vehicle also had four-wheel drive and was powered by a heavy-duty gasoline engine which prevented it from getting stuck in hazardous places and rough conditions. The rugged tires on this vehicle numbered six with four being on the back and two on the front. The heavy tread on each of the tires enabled this vehicle to go on most any type of terrain that they would encounter in their many upcoming battles.

> "They were made to rough it and they were pretty easy to handle. It was basically like driving a big car. These cars weren't armored like the ones we would eventually get when we got into Europe. They were more of a civilian vehicle but still US Army issued and much like a really big powerful jeep."

The daily routines at Camp Livingston were mostly basic military drills for the ones that weren't driving the tanks. With more time spent in this camp than any of the others, the men were now more familiar with the overall tank operations and ready to move onto their next camp and the next specialized phase of their invaluable military training.

Camp Hood was the next stop for this newly formed tank destroyer unit. Each of the men loaded up into their respective vehicles and headed west to the great state of Texas! This stop, now known as Fort Hood, would only last for about six weeks and would be another important training ground for their working knowledge of proper tank combat operations.

> "Didn't have too much for me to do there except more basic training. My duties were not just for Captain Gallagher, but it now included duties for about five other officers from some of the other companies. I got to fire different guns and continue to learn more about the maps we would count on when we were driving in Europe. That was more suited for what my job would be like, map training each and every day!"

Several mock battles between the companies and many ten mile hikes were all part of the routine at this particular military camp. The men were always in full gear with their rifles in hand. They did anything they could as training officers to get these men ready for what they would encounter when in Europe. Hard physical training and hard mental training alike were a new way of life to these boys of this tank destroyer unit.

> "We had guys dropping out because of the heat and the long distances they hiked. Some had to be picked up along the way in an ambulance. These exercises were to see if you could stand the pressure physically and mentally of walking and fighting over such a long distance."

Mr. Libby had made mention of his sworn duty to his position in the unit and the fact that he was to do a good job, allowing *nothing* to affect his ability to do so. Self-discipline, integrity and duty to his country were always high on his list of attributes and he is still proud of this to this day. A story that rang true to this way of thinking was relayed to me by Mr. Libby that would prove this way of thinking to be note-worthy. This is also a slightly humorous tale from his memory but non-the-less, a testament of service first and personal pleasures on the back-burner. Here is his description as it was told to me during one of my many interviews with Mr. Libby.

Integrity, honor and a little *protect your butt*; all needs to be worked into your being when you wear the uniform of any branch of the US military. During the hard, rigorous work and constant training for any GI, there are the down times when you eat, write letters home or just spend time relaxing to chat with the guys within your unit or perform any other duties which are required of you at the base camp aside from your normal routine. Mr. Libby, as was previously mentioned, became an orderly for one of the captains. Captain Gallagher was a man of authority and a well-liked and respected man among the GI's of this unit. Referred to as *dog robbers*, the orderlies were always there to help out their commanding officers. The term dog robber was a term that originated in the first world war which loosely describes the closeness and the loyalty that each orderly must show to their officer as they take care of them day in and day out.

From time to time, Captain Gallagher would ask for minor details to be taken care of along the way for other captains that may need assistance and he would tack on little requests for an orderly with his direct permission. A strong memory of such a time involving the young Charles which goes hand-in-hand with the quality of integrity and honor occurred one day as the visiting wife of an officer requested Charles to come to her residence on base to assist her with an unspecified chore. The chore was of a personal matter and placed him in what he referred to as *"in a pickle"*.

She had seen young Charles around the compound in Texas at Camp Hood and had developed a personal interest in Charles. Her request was for Charles to come and assist her with the preparation of a mixed drink that she wanted prepared by nobody other than the young Charles Libby. Obeying the orders and requests of his superior, Charles reported to the room to find that this request was more of a personal desire to have him there alone with her. At the appropriate time, the young lady embraced Charles and seductively kissed Charles on the lips. Now once again, remember at this time of Charles's youth and looks, the ladies were attracted to the similarities of screen actor Errol Flynn whom he very closely resembled. Mr. Libby remarks that he also found her to be quite beautiful as well and was taken completely off-guard by the advance of this officer's wife. But, as a man of good character, integrity, honor and recognizing that he needed to implement a high dose of *protect your butt*, Charles asked her not to continue with her advancements and seductive actions. Also thinking that if another officer or worse yet, her husband, were to walk into the room, in his words, his butt would be mud! Charles then told her, "I'll fix your drink for you ma'am, but right after that, I'm leaving!"

Later that same week, she requested another visit from young Charles. After arriving, she made her way close to him again to try her luck once more with a seductive kiss. Mr. Libby recalls that he quickly grabbed her by her arms to stop her advance and said . . .

```
"Honey, please don't do this. They'll court-
marshal me and put me in the jug and I'll
never get out until the war is over and I
don't want that to happen. Please stop!"
```

After that incident, she never requested him to come to her quarters and respected his wishes and the caliber of man that Charles was for not compromising his duty to his unit as well as his integrity with married women. Shortly afterwards, the officer's wife went home and the camp for Charles, was back to normal without the beautiful temptress nearby.

Camp Bowie was the next stop in Texas for these boys to acquire some added basic training. Extra knowledge in helping or aiding in whatever your fellow soldiers needed was drilled into the boys of this unit. This was just another stop in this big state for a unit of boys that were rapidly becoming tougher, more mature and hardened military soldiers.

> "Not as nice as the other places we had been to, but we didn't stay there too long for it to make a difference or wear on us. We were there to do a job and we always did it well."

A train was the next form of transportation for the unit to their next testing grounds which was Camp Gordon Johnston, FLA. The unit's vehicles were loaded onto a train to save on time and fuel. All of their vehicles accompanied the men on their journey to the east. This camp provided the men with water training in areas such as swimming and any other type of life saving exercises needed in the event of any water emergency.

> "We didn't stay there very long. It was only about three weeks of water training. We all watched a lot of movies that instructed us in many different situations which would save yourself or your swim buddy in an emergency. Commando self-defense training was also a standard routine there and wasn't too hard for me. We never knew if we would use it but it was there if we needed it."

Another long train ride back to the west of Florida took the tank men of the 628th to a place at that time called Camp Rucker, Alabama.

> "No tanks went on this trip, just our other military vehicles. We didn't know what

> happened to the tanks at the time but we later found out that they were getting ready to go overseas on a ship."

War games were the main activity at Camp Rucker. These war games got more serious due to the limited time that the men had remaining before their trip across the Atlantic Ocean. The use of half-tracks and weapons carriers was the new focus for proper operation and complete understanding of their handling and overall versatile capabilities.

The half-track was a vehicle that had two wheels located in the front and a caterpillar track system on the rear much like that of a large tank. It seated between thirty five to forty men which was a valuable number of soldiers being transported to any location. Many more than that would throw the caterpillar off its wheel operations. The vehicle moved at a much slower speed than some of the others the unit had at its disposal, but was still quite maneuverable in its operations. The use of this vehicle was important in radio activities due to the additional antennas that were attached to the vehicle itself. The half-track played a very important role in the European Theater and proved to be a valuable tool for many combat situations.

Weapons carriers were a vehicle to haul supplies, gasoline, arms and ammunition. These smaller vehicles had four wheel drive and could get into places that larger vehicles could not maneuver into. They were just another great addition to the arsenal of vehicles that would prove to be so valuable to the men of this unit when they finally reached the European Theater of operations.

> "I saw that A and B Company had some motorcycles that ran around the camp. One of the drivers was a hotshot and ended up laying the bike down on his leg from going too fast through some loose gravel. They asked

> me if I wanted to drive one and I told them no way! When I got to Europe I saw the bikes running messages from HQ to the commanders when they didn't want it broadcasted over the radios. There weren't too many of them but the ones that we had were real important to us."

A short drive to Lebanon, Tennessee was the next stop for the boys to continue their training maneuvers. Increased specialized training with their vehicles was on the agenda for this tank unit. Crossing bodies of water and forging new roads as well as the fast construction of temporary bridges all played a major part of their time spent there in Tennessee. The Army Corps of Engineers was attached to this unit to teach the combat soldiers the necessary skills which were needed to forge a temporary bridge over a river if there was no other way to cross that particular body of water. Cable systems, pontoon bridges and understanding depths and shallow spots to safely cross were all involved in this important type of training. This unit had to know how to get *all* of their equipment across a river quickly and safely no matter what!

> "If the battle was *over there*, you had to *get there*. This knowledge proved to be very valuable when we were in Europe near the Rhine River. Each of our tanks moved across these pontoons one at a time. The weight was too great to move any more than that at once. We didn't have to cross too many like that over there, but we knew what to do on the few that we did have to cross. If they located a shallow spot, we wouldn't even bother putting up a pontoon; we'd use that shallow area instead to save us valuable time."

Tennessee maneuvers were an important step in training these young tank destroyers. Conditions were close to what they would encounter and seemed to have many activities that were much like actual combat conditions they later experienced.

> "In Tennessee, bugs were limited and it made it a lot nicer because of the cedar trees. Other places like Louisiana weren't so nice. Wet and hot! We had a guy have a centipede crawl into his ear when we were there and he had to be taken to the nearest hospital. He was kicking and fighting and damn near went crazy. Later they got everything taken care of and he turned out to be alright. You never knew what you were going to see in these strange places."

One day Charles and some other soldiers were in a weapons carrier going over a hill and word came down from a radio that the Japanese Empire had bombed Pearl Harbor. This news rang loudly in the ears of these boys that would be going off to war very soon.

> "One of the guys on the vehicle said, *well here we go!* Later on we were all glad that we didn't go to that part of the war. We all wanted to go to Europe because we had put so much time into training for that."

Two and a half months of war games and training was all that there was time for there in Tennessee. Onto the next stop for this unit which kept on the move much like they would be doing in the very near future. But, first things first, young Charles had a driver's license, he drove one of the company command cars, but had never driven a tank. One day on some free time a good friend of young Charles, a motor pool mechanic and tank operator, asked Charles if he would like to get some valuable driving training on the tank that he may need if asked or forced to perform this duty in combat. Edward Bik took Charles to a nearby training field and got to work with Charles on that calm Sunday afternoon. Charles climbed down into the tank and everything began with simply learning how to get the tank started. After the tank was warmed up and ready to roll, Charles listened to every helpful command from his pal who he called Bik.

US manuevers and some valuable map training which was crucial for any driver in WWII.

"He said that I did very well for not ever driving a tank before. Only one little mistake as I hit a small ditch while doing about 15 miles per hour and hit my chin hard on the padding where you crawl into the tank. It seemed to be pretty easy for me since I was used to driving a truck. Now that I had this tank knowledge, if they needed me to

> take over for a dead tank driver, I could do it. I thought it was very exciting and I thought that I was a big shot."

Back to Fort Rucker, Alabama for some more basic training, map reading skills, 40MM gun operations and some good old fashioned guard duty. The routine became a little more normal for this unit and all of the work became second nature. The next stop was onto Camp Pickett, Virginia and then off to Bradford, Virginia for more basic training, war games, map reading and some more winter survival training. These were all short spurts back and forth and then off to Davis, West Virginia for similar winter training. The pace became faster and the training became more intense as the men themselves could feel the tension that was in the air with the officers and their personal knowledge of what they were close to doing as a tank destroyer unit.

> "The officers, they would talk among themselves and they would keep it quiet from all of us but we all knew what was going on anyway. We knew that it was getting very close for us to go."

The next stop was Fort Dix, New Jersey. Unknown to the regular GI's of the unit, this was to be their final stop in preparing to go overseas. The men were told to take care of all their equipment, machine guns and other rifles which were to be in proper working order. All of their gear which they were to carry onto the ship for their journey had to be ready before leaving the shores of the United States. Still, all the while, they had felt a sense of the urgency. Their superiors there in New Jersey had not yet told them that they were only one step away from climbing aboard that big ship.

> "They told us that it was alright to go into town for a little while. We had a truck that took us there and they told us that they'd

pick us up at nine o'clock that night. We had just got paid the day before so we had some money to spend. I got a steak dinner with mashed potatoes, peas and corn. I even bought the guy sitting next to me dinner who looked like he was hungry and didn't have any money. He told me, soldier, I hope that you get home ok, shook my hand and then I left to get into the military truck to head back to the base."

The men were only there for about two weeks. Classes in map reading and procedure for properly destroying classified information if you had fallen into the enemies hands were all on the agenda here at Fort Dix. After the first week of their time there, the boys of the 628th were all quarantined to the base by strict orders handed down from HQ.

"We knew then that we were going to Shanks to ship out. It was pretty obvious that our next stop was to get on the big ship. They didn't want anyone skipping out or going over the wall so to speak. One guy got scared and went into the latrine and poured a can of lye into his canteen and drank it! They took him to the local hospital and he never shipped out to Europe. We all found out later that he destroyed all of his taste buds but lived through his terrible meltdown and sad ordeal."

At the completion of the two weeks of their training there, the boys were called to order and all marched to the commands of their superiors and were loaded into large personal trucks with all of their gear in tow and drove toward their last stop here in the United States, Camp Shanks, New York.

There they were, ready to board the ship and head across a body of water that would lead them to their destiny and the place that they had been hearing about for months and months each and every day. Camp Shanks was a harbor base and known as the embarkation center which the United States military used as their *shipping out* location on the eastern coast of the United States for departing soldiers and equipment.

```
"When we got there, we unloaded everything
and stood around for about three hours.
We were in our fatigues and ready to get
on the ship. Nothing was said to us but we
knew what was taking place. As I stood there
waiting to get on the ship I thought to my-
self that if I'm going to go into battle,
I'll do my best. No turning back now!"
```

Mr. Libby also remembers that there was a large group of American citizens waiting there to waive to everyone and wish them all well before they boarded the ship. This was a good feeling for the soldiers at the time to know that they had the support of the American people and that they took the time to come and see them off. This is a fond memory for Mr. Libby still to this day seeing all of those people waiving and yelling at all of the soldiers while throwing them kisses. The boys loaded into the ship R.M.S. Aquitania one by one and were each assigned to their own hammock. This was it, the beginning of our boys becoming men! To walk into that ship and start their adventure into the unknown was an act of courage that is undeniably an act that most people could not even begin to think about doing. But this is a group of Americans who had more to prove than just how brave they were. This was a group of boys that didn't just have something to prove to themselves, they had to prove something to the entire world! Their act of courage was an act of kindness for every American who stayed here enjoying their comforts of home and to every citizen of any country across the European continent that felt the sting of the German armies. It was basically a battle between right and wrong, good and evil and a time that the world as we knew it was in complete turmoil. These boys knew what they were doing and did it without blinking an eye. Here we come Europe, here we come!

Charles Libby dressed out in combat gear, somewhere in European Theater.

Shipping Out Europe, Here We Come!

* * *

The Americans are over-paid, over sexed and . . . they're over here! A catch phrase that Mr. Libby remembers fondly as spoken by an English officer upon their arriving in England. This tone-setting comment that rang loudly within the ears of every American GI which was taken lightly as a playful gesture of welcoming these brave soldiers to their soil. A sign of a relationship that would form between the British troops, their citizens and the United States of America, which still stands as a strong bond to this very day. Help came in many forms and as our troops arrived on their shores. A huge sigh of relief came over these men as American soldiers, in a gesture of solidarity, took to their shores ready to attack the demons head-on, which were rapidly making their way toward the British and the now present American troops.

Prior to his deployment to England, Mr. Libby had never been out of the United States. He fondly recalls the long trip as an exciting adventure and also remembers the almost ten thousand men that he was with during this trip across the Atlantic Ocean. All the men were American GI's who were going over to serve this great cause. The boys came from all over our great country with many different family backgrounds, ethnic heritage, skin colors and religious beliefs but had one common factor between them, all of these boys and men were doing this to protect the very freedoms that we all enjoy still to this day. Infantry, anti-tank, artillery gunners, doctors, field medics, chaplains and every type of our trained military might were loaded into that big boat and together headed across the ocean for the same reasons, to defeat a tyrant and rid the world of a great form of evil that was spreading everywhere like a deadly plague.

Bumpy seas and plenty of ocean swells meet these boys on this journey toward their destiny. When asked if Mr. Libby got sea sick, he replied that he didn't, *that time*. His future gunner on his command car from New Jersey, Edward Bik, was not as fortunate. Mr. Libby told me of his friend's humorous and personal battle with sea sickness. Young Charles and Bik had both gone to the canteen at the base in New York and purchased about six O-Henry candy bars each for the long voyage. With a snicker and big smile on his face, he furthers his story by recalling all of the boys that turned white along the way and that Bik was really sorry that he had eaten all of those candy bars. The boys all slept in their assigned hammocks with their personal gear stowed underneath. In the rough seas, these form of beds would swing side to side making it hard for the boys to sleep and also helped along the effects of getting sea sick. Mr. Libby vividly remembers one morning on the ship that he went to awaken Bik and found him still in his swinging hammock looking very sick to his stomach. He described him as having watering eyes and looking sicker than a dog. Charles was eating an O-Henry candy bar at the time as Bik looked up to young Charles who had a huge smile on his face and said,

"Libby, are you really eating an O-Henry?" Libby replied, *"Yeah, you want a bite?"* After offering him some, Bik angrily replied to Charles, "You better get out of here or I'll kill you! Get the hell away from me you son-of-a-bitch!" With a full laugh and a big smile on his face, Mr. Libby seemed to really enjoy telling that particular story about a friend of his during his time of sea sickness. It was my perception from watching him and listening to the story, at that particular time, it was one of the happier times that they spent together. They were just days away from seeing, hearing and smelling the battle grounds of a war where it would prove to be the last steps, sights and breaths that many of these ten thousand boys would spend alive.

"There were only twelve toilets on the ship and every one of them was full at all times from soldiers puking and crapping from the rough seas. Some were even doing their job in the liners of their helmets when all twelve were full. Many of them were sitting on the crapper and throwing up in their helmets at the same time! When I saw that, I got the hell out of there because I didn't want to get sick myself. And my buddy Bik, well he was sick almost the entire way over there."

This feeling of sickness was partially from the waves, swells, thunderstorms, heavy cold rain and partially from the overwhelming fear of the unknown which the boys all felt within the bottom of their stomach. This was a feeling which they had never felt before in their young lives and one that many of them would have to get used to feeling all the time once they did finally arrive!

After getting into what are to be considered international waters, the soldiers were alerted that there was something in the water much more dangerous than anything they had planned for, a submerged German submarine that was following their every movement. After nine days of travel, the soldiers could see the riffles within the currents of the water from their stern side that they were indeed being followed. This caused many of them great concern. Mr. Libby also remembers that the ship had to take a type of zigzag pattern to get to their final destination as not to allow the German submarine to ever get a straight and clear shot at their large vessel which carried this precious payload of soldiers. This slowed the time down considerably as to their intended arrival date on the European continent. Fortunately for the ten thousand men on this ship, the sub never had an opportunity to fire on them and disappeared soon before they reached the beautiful shores of Scotland.

When asked further about Europe, England or any part of that world, Mr. Libby does recall one of his earliest memories about the war or anything to do with the conflict that he was about to enter which had to do with the Russians. His opinion of them at the time was that they were very bold, cocky and that they seemed to always want to start something or to pick a fight with everyone. After arriving in the European Theater of action and interacting at times with Russian soldiers, he found that his preconceived notions were to be true and that they were indeed very difficult soldiers to work and to get along with.

```
"They were bold as hell and really wanted to
pick a fight with the United States and any
of us that were fighting over there. They
thought they won the WWII over there by
themselves. That's just not true! We could
have kicked their asses! I never really cared
for them while I was there but I knew that
I had to get along with them, so I did."
```

Upon arrival in the harbor, the soldiers were greeted with severe sleet and cold blowing rain. With the announcement coming through a loud speaker, "*628th Tank Destroyer Unit, get ready to disembark!*", the soldiers prepared themselves by gathering their rifles and full packs to leave the ship and step onto the docks at this once far away port. Many of the sickened soldiers found this command one of the happiest that they ever heard during their service to their country. So with the command to leave the ship that they had been on for almost ten long days, each of the soldiers in A, B and C-Company moved to one side of the ship to assemble in proper military formation. The remaining forces went to the other side to disembark with their respective commanders for their orders.

After disembarking, the men assembled on the dock in true military formation to receive their first orders on these foreign shores. Sgt. Luckey received commands from five higher officers consisting of Captain William Gallagher, Lieutenant Feldman and three other higher ranking officers of A, B and C-Company. At this point in time, Lt. Colonel Hernandez was the highest officer in charge of the 628th Tank Destroyer Battalion and handed down the orders to Captain Gallagher himself. The boys were instructed to stand along a long stone constructed wall on the banks of the port in a relaxed manner referred to as parade rest. Now, after spending nine long days and nights on a ship and crossing a turbulent ocean, the boys had to wait for almost three full hours for the train that would be transporting them to a station between the cities of Birmingham and Coventry, England. Cold rain, sleet and heavy fog were not the types of greetings that young Charles had expected to find after his long and arduous journey.

For the boys of the 628th, it was off to the British camp Packington Park on a train to stage for the pending large-scale American invasion. Unknown to the boys just when it would take place, they were instructed to keep all of their gear well maintained and to always be at a heightened alert. A lot of waiting around at this point until they were needed, Mr. Libby comments on this nervous time of his life. . .

```
"They knew we were coming, the Germans did,
but they didn't know just when we would
all be there and just how many of us there
would be."
```

This particular camp was described by Mr. Libby as being much like a concentration camp with dirty rooms painted in a dull gun powder gray color. Not very nice compared to what they were all used to in all of the camps that they had been to in the US for the past couple of years while preparing to come over there.

```
"We didn't like it there at that camp very
much but we had to get used to it. The third
night we were there, German planes went over
us on their way to bomb London. You could
```

see the flashes from the bombs exploding when you looked off in the distance toward the city. The air raid sirens sounded so weird and they would go off sometimes all night long! When you heard the sirens, you quickly headed to the bomb shelters because you knew that the Germans were on the way from the air. When the all clear signal was given to us, it was time to leave the tunnels that they had dug out for the shelter. This took a little getting used to. I do give credit to the British soldiers that would get the big spotlights on the German planes. One would locate them and then there would be dozens of lights shining into the air. Then you would see the tracers from the big anti-aircraft guns shooting them down or hitting them hard enough to cause smoke to come out of them and then they would disappear as they tried to get back to Germany."

Trying to get as comfortable as possible, one of the men from the unit decided that he would like to have something more comfortable to sleep in. He knew of a rain cape that was used in WWI used by the Brits. An antique shop had a surplus of these capes and sold them cheap to the American GI's. In turn, they took the capes and their blankets to a local cobbler and he sewed the two together, making a sort of early type of sleeping bag. This bag kept the soldiers not only warmer but also kept them dry with the cape portion. These creative soldiers appreciated that they now had something that was more comfortable and fucntional at night.

"We called them *fart sacks*. We would crawl into them at night and pull the sack over

our heads and would sleep comfortably. The
only worry was that a patrol would be able
to sneak up on us at night and we might not
be able to hear them coming when we were all
zipped up."

Additional training from the British commandos was hand-to-hand self-defense for up close fights that may occur when in combat. Other training dealt with the possibility of being captured and taken prisoner by the Germans or any other axis forces and what type of military procedures were involved in handling these unfortunate and dangerous types of situations.

"We were told what information we were allowed to disclose and what you were never
to tell them, especially any locations of
troops. Any type of identification or sensitive material like photos or maps was never
to be on your person if you were caught. We
kept most of that in our duffle bags down
in the very bottom under our clothing and
they stayed in the vehicles most of the
time."

The anticipated introduction of the M-36 tank along with new tank training and instruction came at this point for the 628th. This unit was the first to use this particular tank in warfare and proved it to be the best on these battlefields! Since WWII, this same tank has been used in many wars by our troops, but the 628th were the guys chosen for the job to test her out first!

"Our guys were excited to drive this new
tank. They especially liked that it was gasoline powered and more maneuverable. We were
afraid that we were going to get the M-10

```
again while we were in Europe. We were glad
to be the first ones to have this tank and
I am glad that they still use it today. They
were the best on the battlefield for sure!"
```

For Mr. Libby, command car driver, his duties were limited to this area of Packington Park. The duties of the drivers, mechanics and infantry were enhanced as they learned what they needed to move onto the battles that they would soon see. Nerves certainly had to be settled in these fresh soldiers. The unknown of what was ahead of them was an experience that would make anyone ponder their future and whether they would live or die. With stories starting to come through the grapevine of the killing of Jews, this point in the service of Charles was disturbing to him. Trickling information about these horrendous events were kept away from the soldiers as to not spook them or keep them from losing their nerve. Charles caught wind of it there in England and kept it to himself during his journeys.

For the young Charles Libby, it was business as usual and an adventure that he would embrace with courage day in and day out as he too prepared to make the dangerous journey into the battlefields of Europe, but not before a brief stay in a British hospital.

A reoccurring bout with boils that had started popping up on his legs and buttocks during the US maneuvers, kept Charles Libby in a military hospital for nearly a week. Doctors wanted to make sure that these freshly lanced boils would not get infected and cause him more trouble while in battle. During his brief stay, Charles could hear the sounds of bombers going over and striking the lines of the Germans prior to the invasion at Omaha Beach.

```
"It was like a highway in the sky. They'd
start at two in the morning and still be
going strong at twelve noon! I could see
them from my wing of the hospital and when
```

> the planes would fly over us, it would break some of the glass out of the windows from the pressure. There would be one line of planes flying to to drop their payload and another coming back in to refuel and get more bombs for hours at a time. When a bomb would go off close to the hospital, it would pick us up off of the bed and put us on the floor. That was a scary thing to live through as a fresh young soldier."

Barrage balloons which resembled German blimps flew over London, England and other major British cities, helped to hide targets and to make it that much harder for the German Luftwaffe to bomb these important and highly populated cities.

> "The British used to say that the balloons were there holding Britain up because of all the Americans that were there on the island. We thought it was funny and never said anything back to them about it. We knew that they were glad that we were all there to help them out."

Metal nets also hung from the bottom of these large balloons in an effort to snag planes that may try to come below the level of the balloon itself. Although Mr. Libby had never seen one of these planes do such an uncalculated maneuver, he had heard that it did happen to some of the German planes and successfully stopped them from releasing their deadly payload of bombs and bullets.

A doctor came to Charles and asked him if he would like to stay back to continue his treatments under their care and ride out later with another unit. Charles told the doctor that he would rather go with his own unit and be with the boys that he had been training with for all these months. The doctor did the necessary paperwork and released Charles so that he could return to his active duties as the lead Command Car driver of C-Company. The boils healed up just after their invasion of Omaha beach and Charles was on his way into action and ready for what the war was about to throw at him . . . *From the Command Car.*

Our Weapons and Gear

* * *

Superior firepower, superior maneuverability, superior handling and a little bit of luck went a long way when facing off against the enemy that had plenty of valuable time to become completely entrenched and comfortable with their strategic positions. This was a time of American manufacturing and ingenuity that drew the entire country into their need for precious metals to provide our servicemen with many powerful weapons that would withstand the might of the German army. A true need for a more powerful tank existed and the American workforce as well as the skilled engineers of the United States Army would come through with the development of not only a better tank, but also better ammunition to be used against the tough and proven regiments of German Tiger and Panther tanks.

At Fort Hood, Texas they had the M-10 tank destroyer which had the 3-inch gun motor carriage. This was a diesel fueled machine that burned the eyes of the soldiers and affected their breathing. It was not at all healthy and could affect their overall performance during battle. Upon arriving in Wales, the unit was switched to the M-36 Tank that was fueled by regular gasoline, which in turn was easier on the lungs and eyes of the soldiers who would be around these tanks day-in and day-out during combat. This tank was also much more powerful and had a more considerable amount of firepower and sophistication and was appreciated by the men who operated it. The 90mm gun motor carriage M-36 would get tested by these tank destroyers of the 628th for the first time in actual combat. American ingenuity would be put on display for the entire world to see through its might and powerful weapon that they armed their soldiers with.

The ammunition of this tank was also something that would be feared by the German troops. This armor-piercing round after hitting its intended target, would bore itself into the wall of the enemy tank and with the release of pressure upon its entry of the tank compartment; would detonate, killing everyone that was inside. This ammunition round was also a quieter round than the German tank shells. When fired by the M-36, it provided an advantage to the Americans in detecting its true location of delivery.

> "When you would here the German tank shells coming, they made a sharp sounding sizzle that told you that you better get down or behind something fast! Our shells had a much smoother sound through the air. When ours hit, if the top of the tank didn't blow off, shrapnel and flesh would be all over the inside of the tank compartment when we looked inside. Fire would escape from the turret and more shrapnel would come out of any opening the tank had. It was truly an incredible thing to see. You couldn't get scared when you saw that stuff or think about getting killed or you would never survive the stress that you put on yourself."

Your equipment and your vehicle were just like a part of your body and your portable rolling home away from home. Time spent within your vehicle as a driver was something that had to become comfortable and second nature to you. Just as you become comfortable and feel safe within your very own home, a command car driver needed to feel the same as he sat within this armored vehicle. Day after day as he drove this piece of machinery, a command car driver would understand all of its capabilities and all of its limitations. How fast it would move, how much of an angle it could withstand, what type of surfaces it could maneuver through and what type of arms fire it could protect its personnel when under attack all came into play.

The M-20 Armored Command Car. Charles Libby (top) with two fellow C-Company soldiers.

Charles drove the **M20 Armored Command Car** which protected himself, his radio / gunner and most importantly, the officer who Charles was transporting at that time. These innovative vehicles were four-wheel drive with double axils and six deep tread tires which enabled the driver to go through mud, water and other hazardous road and trail conditions with great maneuverability and made much less noise than any of the half-tracks, tanks and even the jeeps that were rolling through each and every battle.

```
"Captain Jones told me to take the front
fenders off of the command car because the
mud was building up on top of the tires and
would slow it down. I took a chisel and a
hammer and cut them off where they joined
the body. This was done when we were out in
combat so the fenders were left by the road-
side right where I did the quick removal
job. It seemed to work very well and helped
with our speed and control. Captain Jones
was a pretty sharp man."
```

The engine was located behind the driver's seat and not in the front like most vehicles.

Heavy reinforced iron lined the front of this vehicle to protect against land mines and small arms fire from an approaching enemy. The men climbed over the front of the vehicle into the command car since there were no doors on this vehicle. There were two small steps for your access into this car. From a hinge, an armored plate would be moved into position to protect the driver and the assistant driver if present on the vehicle. The passengers would each position themselves under the armor which also protected the ammunition that was located in the rear of the vehicle. The armored plate in front of the driver which protected him from small arms fire also was equipped with a small window made of bullet-proof glass measuring approximately two inches high and four inches long. The side walls were almost three inches thick and the front was almost four inches thick with the headlights built right into the curvature of the vehicle. Smaller dark blue lights were used as a night light and directional tool for not only yourself but for other vehicles that were close to your position. The blue lights could also help others to determine that you were friend and not foe when approaching one another at night. Controlled by two separate switches in the dashboard, the lights were easily turned on or off by the driver.

> "There were times that I had to drive without my headlights when we thought that there may be Germans in the area. One time I had to use the light from the sky to stay centered on the road. Captain Jones asked me if I could see alright and I told him that I was fine with following the moonlight. He trusted me and we made it through this German hot zone just fine."

Charles knew a liaison sergeant that was an artist who offered to paint a picture on his command car's rear fender area. The picture, a broadside naked woman, became a part of the vehicle and its personality. According to Mr. Libby, everybody knew just who's vehicle it was as it was approaching and it became a sort of talk-of-the-town within the unit.

The command car was fitted with a powerful 50 caliber machine gun which was mounted just behind the driver of this vehicle. It had the ability to maneuver a full 360 degrees. Mr. Libby remembers learning to use this gun properly when he was in Wales. This powerful gun was a very useful tool for this particular vehicle and was operated on Charles's command car by the radio man Peterson. Charles himself never had to live fire this big gun in battle but held the knowledge of its operation in the event he was needed to do so and armed it a couple of times pointing at planes that were in the area of his unit.

> "It would do the job! When something was hit with a round from the 50 caliber, it was dead! Peterson would ring my ears when he'd fire up at oncoming planes because I didn't have anything in my ears at times to protect them from the sound of the big gun."

Radio equipment was installed in these command cars and was attached to a make-shift shelf behind the assistant driver's seat. An long extendable antenna would be raised from the vehicle that was attached to the radio itself and could also be detached. For better reception, this almost four foot telescopic antenna would aid the radio man in receiving valuable information that he would transfer to the officer in charge and others in the unit if necessary.

A fire extinguisher was also a comforting piece of equipment which was mounted near the driver of a command car. Not only used for putting out vehicle fires, the fire extinguishers were a great tool for heating up the distributer to start a cold motor in the frigid temperatures of Europe during the long winter months. This little technique was something that was discovered by another driver and passed onto Charles with much enthusiasm and heart-filled thanks as he needed to be able to start the vehicle in any type of weather conditions as a matter of life or death.

Additional weapons included the M-1 carbine rifle which was standard issued to each of the soldiers as their weapon for close quarters combat. Proper operation of this weapon was vital to their safety and survival. Mr. Libby remembers that some of the boys didn't pay attention during maneuvers to the fact that your fingers would have to be out of the way of the clip and he personally saw some of the boys in his unit get them broken during their training. Charles Libby qualified for his marksmanship with this weapon and fondly remembers that he was very good with this particular style of military issued rifle.

```
"I was pretty good with that rifle. It didn't
seem hard to me and I did what they told me
to do with it. I hunted rabbits when I was
young in the CCC Camp and was very familiar
with shooting rifles."
```

An obstacle course in US maneuvers provided the men with proper handling of the M-1 which was equipped with a bayonet for lunging and stabbing in the event they would encounter the enemy head-on. Straw-filled dummies were the targets for the soldiers to act out their possible battlefield encounters. Barbed wire along the obstacle course had presented other tasks for the men to crawl under while carrying these weapons with training methods used in WWI. Mr. Libby remembers these drills, how they were implemented and how they were to be used in this next world war that he was part of.

The use of the bazooka, mortars and hand grenades were also in the arsenal of the men and Charles had his opportunity to qualify with all of these weapons as well. Remembering the awesome power of the hand held shoulder bazooka, Mr. Libby commented on this weapon . . .

> "One guy shot the weapon on the training course on a downgrade hill and was blown clean back onto his butt. He didn't lean into the weapon enough and it took him for a ride. The drill sergeant just shook his head, smiled and went on with the exercise. The soldier came back up and commented about how hard it kicked. Everybody qualified with the weapon that day except for him."

A metal ammunition box held pumpkin ball grenades within the command car which was kept behind the assistant driver's seat. These were thrown by the gunner into areas where he believed Germans were hiding and many times they were correct in this thinking, killing them almost instantly. Ammunition carriers within the unit would bring replacement grenades and any other types of ammunition that needed to be replaced after encounters with the Germans from ordinance which was always located in the rear echelon.

> "We'd yell at them, do you have any pumpkin balls or any rip cords and they'd tell us what they had and bring us whatever we needed at the time. They were in the rear most of the time away from the front enemy lines. Most all of them were nice fellows and had a lot of respect for the tank men up in the front of the battles."

The proper method of slitting an enemy soldier's throat was also part of his training and each of the soldiers carried a knife with them into battle just for this purpose. Charles himself carried an old hunting knife that his brother-in-law hand-made especially for him. He also carried his bayonet which would also serve in the event of close quarter fighting. This training with the knife was given to the boys during the maneuvers in the US and they were also shown additional techniques from a British Commando soldier upon arriving on their foggy and rainy shores.

> "He was the boss and you didn't fool around during his class. He really knew what he was doing. I didn't much care for him and neither did the other guys, but that was ok. I wasn't there to like him; I was there to learn how to defend myself and to kill the Germans."

After reaching England, Charles was issued a .45 caliber pistol. It was a smarter weapon for anyone in the driver's seat without having as much room for rifle use. A heavy canvas belt full of ammunition called a bandolier, would also be standard for each of the soldiers with the appropriate caliber for their weapon of choice.

> "We didn't mind the extra weight. It would kind of hold in your stomach. But in my armored car I had mine hanging up on a rack. I also traveled with a 9mm carbine rifle and buddy when you lay down to rest; you made sure that your weapon was fully loaded and close to your hip. They weren't as bulky as the M-1 that would bang around in your vehicle."

As well as the necessary weapons, the men had their military ruck sack which held their personal items for their every day needs and the many survival situations. Along with a canteen strapped to their hip, the ruck sack held their mess kit which was used for their meals as well as a small gas stove, a folding shovel and pick axe for digging trenches and vehicle hazards. Also, in a last-ditch effort to survive, this shovel could be used as a fighting weapon. There were wooden matches, lighters, starter fluid and a carton of cigarettes once a month provided by the companies who made them in their sacks as well. Charles, not being a heavy smoker, had saved his and at one point had ten cartons which he fondly remembers selling to the Belgian soldiers for ten dollars per carton.

> "They were very glad to get them and I was glad to have the extra money. I had my own little business going on and always had fun doing it. I didn't need the smokes."

Underwear, undershirts, socks and a sewing kit were also included within these ruck sacks. It was up to the soldiers as to how many they wanted to take and could ultimately fit within this valuable piece of equipment they had with them. Mr. Libby also had a pair of Arctic's to cover his army issued boots which aided in keeping his feet warm and dry in the cold winter months. As the command car driver, Charles wore what they called a combat suit. It was a lined uniform and resembled that of a bib overhaul that many Americans wore as they would farm their land in the country, but this one was a military style. A winter jacket was worn over the uniform as pilots wore with their flight suits which kept him warm enough in the frigid temperatures that he encountered.

New equipment for the command car was added by the United States Army to aid in additional identification of units and vehicles on the ground by American planes from the air. American vehicles would be provided with a series of colored panels which attached to the roof or the vehicle's hood. These square, vinyl, flexible panels came in different colors. The thought process was that troops would change the colored panel each day. All American pilots would know prior to their mission what color ground troops were using that particular day and in turn, would not strafe or bomb the advancing troops. These panels came in such colors as red, pink, white, yellow and pale blue. Charles was responsible for changing these panels on the command car daily. With the call from HQ, the radio man Peterson would instruct him in the color of the day which would protect his vehicle whether he was in the main convoy or if he had to make a run back to the rear echelon or off on any side road. This valuable piece of equipment was something that gave comfort to the ground troops. Mr. Libby commented that these panels must have saved them from friendly fire multiple times.

```
"It was a very good idea. The Germans picked
up on it and tried to copy us but they had
one thing wrong, the paint that they used
didn't have the reflective color in it. The
airmen could tell the difference and were
able to sort them out just from that. They
saved our butts many times!"
```

Command car drivers like Mr. Libby were issued a pair of heavy-duty rubber face goggles that kept the road dirt and other small flying objects from getting into his eyes and impairing his vision when the plate metal wasn't in place. He still has these issued goggles to this day and stated that they were a very important tool in his driving.

10-in-1 rations was the name of the actual food issued to each of the soldiers. Tanks and supply trucks all carried a wealth of these rations for the soldiers. Oatmeal cookies with other mystery ingredients which the boys referred to as *hard tack*, due to the hardness of these treats, were just one of the items within these precious food rations.

> "They were pretty hard to chew at times, but they were a pretty good little snack and we all looked forward to having one with our meals."

Containers of corned-beef hash and a one pound can of bacon were also items included in the rations menu. The soldiers were known to save the remaining bacon fat in a glass jar to cook their eggs in at a later time to add additional flavoring. Command car drivers were responsible for the amount of food that they had on their car to feed the officer who they were driving through the battles. In the case of Charles Libby, he was in charge of a captain and a radio man.

A strong memory comes from a situation where a second lieutenant would come to his command car for food when they would stop for a break from the action to eat a quick meal. This particular officer thought that he would be able to eat from the same food that the captain was getting from his command car driver. After a few times of this happening, Charles became increasingly agitated as to the amount that he was consuming and was concerned that he would have to take away from his radio man and the captain himself to feed this moocher. Trying to push his rank and weight around with Charles didn't settle well with him when he had a job to do and was responsible for the entire well-being of the men on his car each and every day. He then thought it best to address the matter to the captain himself.

> "I told him, Captain, this young second lieutenant is coming over here for every meal and I'm getting pissed off that I have to feed him and all I've got is enough for the three of us on this vehicle."

The captain addressed his concerns by telling him to say something to the other officer the next time he came over to eat from the limited supply of food that they had on their car. At next meal, the second lieutenant once again came over to have Charles include him in their meal. Charles looked at him and said,

> "Lieutenant, I have enough stuff to feed Captain Jones, my radio officer and myself. I don't have enough to short-cut them every time we stop to feed you too. I'd appreciate it if you would go to Sgt. Luckey on his supply truck and eat with them."

The young and bold lieutenant looked at Charles as if he was angry that a lower-ranked soldier was talking to him like that. He then looked at the captain for some reply and got nothing but an unconcerned look. The captain was behind Charles and knew that he had spoke up to better take care of his men that depended on him to perform the duties of a command car driver. The officer could say nothing and went on his way to eat with the other men.

> "I only had to tell him once and he never came back. Boy he was mad that a lower ranking soldier got one over on him. I had a job to do and needed to do it properly, nothing personal against him."

Food was the one thing that brought pleasure to these men while they were away from their comfortable homes in the United States. Food was also the item that kept them physically strong and enabled them to keep their fighting spirit that they needed in the cold winters and any other conditions that would certainly make them weaker if they became ill due to an improper diet. This was important to Charles and he certainly was going to do whatever he could to make sure that they would have what they needed until they were resupplied again which sometimes could take several days in a heavily fortified area.

Times have certainly changed with computers, laser-guided weapons, drones and the many technological advancements that the US military has at their disposal today. The weapons and gear of WWII seems almost archaic as we look at the old film footage and hear their stories. But as Mr. Libby has stated to me many times over, the weapons did the job! They had to make it work and they did just that. These men were the *testers* if you will for many of the weapons that we use now, the predecessors to our technology we now know as superior. These men fought with what they were given and trusted that it would keep them alive. For many, it did and they fought using them until the day they were loaded back onto a ship and made the long voyage back across the ocean to the shores of the United States of America. Many of these weapons, vehicles, survival tools and personal items are displayed in museums, memorials and can be found in the homes of many surviving soldiers of this war as well as the relatives that they passed them down to. These items are all an important piece of history and each one tells its own unique story. Preservation of such items should be at the forefront of historians as a constant reminder of how far we have come, of what we used to win a world war and most importantly, as to what we need to do and look for to prevent another event like the entire world painfully took part in.

Our Path to the Germans

✳ ✳ ✳

"It was postponed about three times that I can remember. The weather was really bad, the water was choppy and Eisenhower postponed the invasion to try and save American soldiers from dying. We all thought that we were going to go in there on the first wave, but they had to hold us back, the 628th, because they had to have a beach-head so that we could get all of our tanks safely on the shore. When we finally got there, Oh my God! It was a sight to see, the sight of death everywhere. Not all the bodies were gone yet, the water was still bloody and the smell was terrible!"

THIS WAS AN INITIAL MEMORY of the 628th path to the Germans from Mr. Libby. And so, with the order of the commander and chief and a short trip from Dorchester, England across the English Channel, they were off to their first destination at Omaha Beach which was the start of their direct path to meet the Germans head-on. This arrival of the 628th was only five days after the initial bloody and most famous joint invasion by the US and English troops. As Mr. Libby stated, they needed to properly prepare everything so that the tank unit could safely enter the beach and take their new strategic positions without additional risks to the large tanks and the men themselves who would be operating them. They knew that these fighting machines would be one of the most valuable assets on the ground to win this war and every single precaution was taken to protect each and every one of them.

Referring back to Mr. Libby's previous story of the soldiers who got sick coming across the Atlantic to get to Scotland, Mr. Libby comments that this particular ride across the English Channel was the first time that he himself felt ill from the choppy sea waters and their churning motion. Sitting on the forward plate metal of his command car while being transported, the feeling hit him hard. He commented that he became very dizzy and that he felt as if he was going to actually pass out. The boys and their vehicles were all loaded onto this LST, which basically means a landing ship for troops and tanks. They all braved the choppy waters with their wealth of might, machinery and human assets to do battle on this large transport vessel.

"When they open the doors of the LST, you don't wait! You don't wait for orders to get off, you go! I drove my vehicle about thirty yards before finally reaching the beach. It was a good thing that the water wasn't any higher that day or high waves in the section where we landed or we all would have certainly drowned. The tanks were behind me in the LST. My command car was the first off into the water and I became the lead vehicle with my radio man Peterson. I don't really know where the officers were at that time. I think they came on another boat, but I know that I didn't have the captain with me at that time. I revved my motor up and spun the tires in the wet sand and as I got closer to the shore I got more and more traction. My command car handled it pretty well. I drove up the beach and drove past two German pill boxes that were blown out. There was one on the right side of me and one on the left. The one on the right sat higher on the beachhead and I saw that our guys had previously blown out the window killing the Germans that were inside. The infantry had cleared the path for us so we didn't run over the dead soldiers and smash their bodies. I looked down the beach and saw a high cliff that soldiers were shooting grappling hooks to the top to climb up to kill some Germans that were up there. Some of our GI's were knocked off of the wall and some others seemed to have made it up there to take care of them. I was safely off of the beach shortly after that."

American LST arriving at Omaha Beach with our brave soldiers.

The beach was bloody from the sand to the water. The horrible smell of death was in the air and they had just gotten there. There was no turning back now! This is what they were trained for and they now had a job to do. Everyone was depending on this tank destroyer unit to be a mighty force in the defeat of the axis powers, especially the German forces of Adolph Hitler.

> "Mortar fire was coming in and some even hit pretty close to me. The sand absorbed most of the impact and it would blow it straight up into the air instead of blasting to the sides. When they hit, they went in really deep. I was told to get off the beach as quickly as I could and get on the high road above the two German pill boxes. We needed to get into position to set up our tanks and stop them while they retreated. They were running fast because we were hot on their tails. Some stayed to fight but they ended up getting killed by our guys. A German pilot made a quick run past us and started strafing into the water. He only made one pass before we all started shooting back at him.
>
> He flew away but not before killing some of our guys. It was the first time I had ever seen anyone get killed, but it certainly wasn't the last time. It was a hell of a thing."

As the men proceeded down their first road toward the enemy approximately five miles from the shores of Omaha Beach, young Charles saw a farmhouse off to the left side of the road. From the doorway of this old farmhouse, there was a woman who was screaming and yelling to the men that were rapidly approaching. This would be the first place that they would see the mind-set, tactics and desperation first hand of the deeply entrenched German army.

> "We didn't know what the heck was going on or what was wrong. Dyda, wanted to be a hotshot so he went up there to see what was going on and found that she had a live trip wire across her doorway. When we saw Dyda reaching for the trip wire, we knew what he was going to try to do and we all yelled don't do it, don't do it Dyda!

The young and inexperienced soldier reached for a pair of snippers out of his pack and cut the live trip wire. When the pressure of the wire was released from being cut, the explosive device swung toward him and got caught in the doorway, fortunately without going off. The boys of the unit came to Dyda's aid and carefully took the explosive device into a nearby field and threw it where it detonated safely away from the farm house, saving it and the woman who lived inside. The now shaking woman gave Dyda a big hug and the soldiers were all on their way back down the long road before they were missed by commanders who were on the road well out in front of them at this point.

There they were, not five miles from their landing on the shores and already a taste of what they were going to be facing. All along the road, the Germans provided some mortar fire at the unit but fortunately for the 628th, they never hit anyone. Mr. Libby remembers that one round hit close to a vehicle and the concussion blew a couple of soldiers out of their seats and they were quickly loaded into an ambulance and taken to the rear echelon and eventually away to a military hospital to get checked out and patched up. But, as far as vehicles and tanks, nothing was lost due to the bad coordinates of the Germans operating the mortar fire that particular day.

Traveling down the road, ever wary of what to expect as a new unit of men on the first leg of the war, the Americans came across several British soldiers in a long trench. As Charles slowed down, he noticed the soldiers sitting there as if they didn't have a worry in the world. An American officer near Charles's vehicle asked these soldiers why they weren't involved in the taking of the town ahead which was assigned to the British forces by HQ.

> "I heard the one British soldier say back to the American officer, we have to have our tea at ten, two and four. They were actually sitting in a trench with water running through it having tea! The officer shook his head and walked away mumbling under his breath that they were drinking tea and we were all the way over here to help them while they drink tea. We all just moved on shaking our heads in wonder and shocked about what we had just seen."

The men of the 628th and all the units that were attached to them soon approached a large cabbage patch which was planted by a local farmer. A German soldier popped up out of the patch after getting too scared from the sounds of the Americans. He threw his hands up into the air and yelled *Comrade!* at the Americans. The 47th infantry men went into the cabbage patch and found another five Germans in there who were also ready to surrender to the American troops. Time was ticking away and the unit had to keep moving toward their first major goal of reaching and liberating the city of Paris, France.

> "Captain Gallagher told us tank guys that if we wanted to capture Germans that we were supposed to go and join the infantry, so we stayed with our vehicles and stayed focused on what our job was. We let the capturing

> of German soldiers up to the infantry guys
> after that day."

Approaching an intersection on this road near the town of Le Mans, France, the boys rolled up on what appeared to be a small pub. Some of the men from the 47th Armored Infantry decided to go into the pub and quickly inspect it. Six of these brave soldiers walked into the pub and to their surprise found four German officers sitting on bar stools not one bit aware or seemingly concerned that they were being approached by these American soldiers.

> "They heard the vehicles and tanks approach-
> ing but thought that it was the German army
> retreating so they didn't give it any thought
> and just sat there drinking, is what we as-
> sumed. They didn't know that we were all
> there now rolling through the streets that
> they thought they had complete control of."

The German soldiers turned to see the Americans standing in front of them with rifles in hand telling them to get their hands up in some broken German. The officers ignored their commands until one of the 47th infantry soldiers chambered a shell, quickly getting the attention of all four of them. Now with a stern command to get their hands up, the German officers did so and were immediately taken outside of the pub to be interrogated and thoroughly searched.

> "We couldn't believe it when they walked
> out with four Krauts! The 47th got their
> pistols, daggers and more importantly some
> documents that they could get information
> about the German battery and where head-
> quarters was located up the road. We were
> only a few miles away from where they were."

The MP's were called by radio and were sent to their location where they picked up this valuable find that our men had taken prisoners. A quick stop at a pub and the capture of four German officers, this was not a bad start so far for the men of these units after being there for such a short time.

> "We had to keep moving along that road, so the other guys took care of the Krauts. Everybody had their own important jobs to do and ours was to keep moving ahead quickly."

Moving forward to get to Paris, the unit approached a small town named Sees. Upon approaching the city, the men were greeted by dozens of residents curious to see the Americans. With great joy that they had finally arrived there to help them, they gave beautiful flowers to the American soldiers as a sign of appreciation. The tanks were ahead of the main unit and were moving cautiously due to not knowing what they would find on this particular road. The high probability of road bombs and additional German troops was always a big threat. So, as the men waited for their orders to move ahead, something changed the peace and quiet of the celebration drastically.

> "All of a sudden at twelve noon, everyone just disappeared. We thought they all went home for dinner, then we found out what it was like to be under heavy German fire. I crawled under my vehicle and knew that it was mortar fire. I stayed under there for more than an hour until the barrage of shelling was over. It seemed like a safe place to be. Then, after it was over, we didn't wait long to get out of there! There were spies all over the place and you never knew who they were. There was probably one in the crowd of people and they tipped off the Germans

> that we were there. A local resident who was not liked in that community was carrying information to the Germans and the other residents found out just then that he was a German sympathizer. An old man about sixty five or seventy years old walked up behind him while this traitor was looking at an American tank. He was carrying a double-barrel shot gun and put it right behind the man's head and pulled the trigger. He blew his brains all over the side of the American tank. The tank sergeant was reloading his 50 caliber gun at the time and saw it all happen. Man he was mad that they had gotten brains all over the side of his tank. We didn't get involved with the affairs of the residents and their communities so they drug the guy away and threw him over a bank and we moved cautiously out of the town, a little more careful and a whole lot wiser!"

Besides the light incoming barrage they encountered getting off of the beach, this would prove to be the first taste of heavy live enemy mortar fire for the 628th and it was certainly a wake-up call for these young, wet behind the ears and unseasoned boys. Hiding under their vehicles and behind anything that would possibly shelter them from the incoming shells directed at them, the boys didn't hear much of anything until the actual explosions as they hit around them. This skirmish that Mr. Libby speaks of would later be known in history as the *Battle of the Seine River* and Mr. Libby lived through it to tell his amazing story.

> "Cowen was another jeep driver that I knew and was friends with. He had gone back to the rear to pick up 10-in-1 rations and other

supplies. On his way back, he got caught in the incoming mortar fire and was hit in the back by shrapnel and it made a big hole. It was bad! It killed him instantly; he didn't know what hit him. He was a funny guy and I was sad that he had gotten it. He was the first in our unit to get killed that I knew of."

On August 20th, Lt. Colonel Hernandez, was killed in action in the city of Douains, France. Hernandez was the commanding officer of the 628th Tank Destroyer Battalion attached to the 5th armored division of the United States Army. A round from an American tank killed him after giving orders to fire the tank's artillery into a German stronghold equipped with 88 calibur cannons. History tells the story of his death in another way, but Mr. Libby remembers what he had heard directly from his unit and what really had happened that day there in France. . .

"Word spread down through our unit like wildfire. It came down on the radio that he had been killed ahead of us. The entire unit was in complete and total shock. Later, I got the real story from the sergeant of the tank that actually fired the round as he told a group of us what had happened as we pulled back to rest. Lt. Colonel Hernandez had given this tank driver his coordinates to fire into the Germans. The tank driver spoke up to Hernandez and told him that there were high tension power lines overhead and that if he followed that order to fire, the round could hit the lines and blow up over them. Colonel Hernandez was mad that the sergeant didn't immediately obey the order and told him that he had given him a direct order and was to fire the exact coordinates that he had requested. Not many of the men liked him because of this attitude and behavior while he was trying to be just like Patton. He was no Patton! So, when the tank driver fired the round as he was ordered, sadly it did exactly what he had predicted and conveyed to Colonel Hernandez. The tank round hit the lines, blew up overhead of them and killed not only Lt. Colonel Hernandez, but also killed his personal driver. We were all shocked that it happened. All he needed to do was to listen to his tank sergeant and he would have been alive. We lost our battalion commander that day and a very good driver as well."

Captain William Gallagher, the officer who Charles drove in his vehicle, was quickly promoted to Lt. Colonel and immediately took over the duties of Lt. Colonel Hernandez at HQ. This was a tremendous responsibility for Captain Gallagher and made Charles very happy that the man he respected so much now had been promoted to a position that would benefit him as a soldier and also to have such a responsible man in a high position to help save American lives while handling the commands of war with precision and a cool head.

Captain Robert Jones would be the next officer that Charles Libby would be responsible for driving into the next phase of the war. Jones came from B-Company and was known by the men of C-Company. They were unsure of what type of leader he would be but it was proven later that he was the type of man that the boys of C-Company would respect and proudly serve under.

> "I was glad that he was the one who got that promotion, Captain Gallagher. He was a very likable guy and always thought a lot of me and always took great care of me as well. I knew that the new guy I would drive was from B-Company. He was made captain after he was moved to our company in the shuffle to get new commanders into the right places. We were all a little worried about him at first but he turned out to be a guy that we all liked very much and respected even more!"

Another unit took care of the cover mortar fire as the 628th moved toward Paris, France. Mr. Libby remembers that he was told that they had blown out the mortars and took care of that one particular stronghold the Germans had. At this point, he also remembered that there were well over a hundred German soldiers killed by his unit on their bloody path toward Paris, France.

> "They wouldn't hesitate to jump right out in front of you while we were driving down the road and just start shooting. We'd have to kill them and as we drove by them we'd say, there lays Fritz. Many of the German prisoners would tell us that they had to fight with honor or die. Hitler would have had them shot for not fighting as hard as they could and they all knew it."

Mr. Libby remembers that not that many from C-Company had lost their lives at this point but from other units, snipers had been successful in taking many of the American soldiers out in that fashion. The men would hear the sound and then follow it to the sniper and take him out. They proved to be a force that was very successful in hurting ground unit numbers and the Americans were always aware of the possibility of coming across more of them along their path.

> "We would drive slowly on our way to Paris not knowing if it was occupied by the Germans. They would hide in church towers, empty water towers or on top of high buildings. Sometimes there were snipers in these places and we would fire an .88 to take them out. Water would run out of the tower and if it was red, we knew that we hit someone that was inside. We encountered Germans the entire way there. Some wanted to keep fighting and others had enough of the fighting and gladly surrendered to us."

Along the path, Germans would be cleaned out and afterwards the residents would come out to greet the Americans with thanks and praise for helping them rid their villages and towns of the invading Germans who had taken control of their very lives. As the final approach to Paris was near, the men of the 628th stopped around ten miles from the main city to regroup and prepare for their entry into the place that they had been moving toward for all this time. A large fountain marked this location which was called *Fountaine Belleaue* and the men found it enticing at this point of their journey. Several women from the village were using the fountain to wash their families clothing. One of the soldiers decided that the fountain was a perfect place to take a bath during this rest period. Stripping down to his birthday suit, the soldier jumped in and started to bathe right in front of the unsurprised French women.

> "When we saw him stripping down and getting into the fountain, about fifteen of us decided that if he was going to do it, why not join him? The women just smiled

and were nice enough to wash our backs. No funny business, just being polite to the American GI's and wanting to help us out. Captain Jones just smiled and shook his head when he saw all of us in that public fountain, completely naked and getting our backs washed."

This particular story presented questions within my mind about the men and their ability to remain clean, both in body and their clothing. A war zone in the 1940's is not exactly the ideal place to find a place to bathe and do your laundry. Constantly on the move, fighting and feeling exhaustion could not have made it easy for these soldiers to remain clean. When asked about this particular situation, Mr. Libby chuckled and described some of the methods and the timing of these personal hygiene issues.

"Ha ha ha, that's a good question! Let's just start by saying that a bath was a luxury that we didn't enjoy on a regular basis. The fountain was certainly a big treat for all of us! In the warmer months of battle, we would use the creeks that we came across during our time of bivouac to wash ourselves and our clothes. If we came across a house that had a fireplace, we would start a fire and then we'd warm up creek water in our helmets and wash our stuff like that. We would do our thing, get as clean as we could and then move out of the house and get back to the vehicles and then down the road. In the colder months, it was much harder to get clean or to clean any of our laundry. We would try to at least wash our underarms

> and our private parts to prevent rash or any types of infections. It wasn't always pleasant being that dirty, but that was war!"

The short-lived break was over for the soldiers of the 628th and they were ready to move forward into the city of Paris smelling much better than just hours before. The 628th was the lead unit into Paris and were accompanied by the 5th Battalion and the 47th Armored Infantry. As the approaching units made their way into the outer city limits, the Germans fled the main parts of the city without a single shot from a gun, a blast from a tank or any type of German opposition.

> "I can remember seeing the Eiffel Tower off to the right side of my vehicle in the distance. The Arc de Triomphe was in front of me. We turned left and were on our new path toward Belgium. There wasn't anyone on the streets where I was at the time. They heard the tanks coming near them and weren't sure if it was the Germans or us. As we moved through, people started to slowly come out of the buildings. We ran into a Belgium guy who was headed home on the road toward Paris and he told us that he had heard that Hitler had plans to blow up the Eiffel Tower. We were happy to be there in Paris and that we possibly saved the famous tower and the Arc de Triomphe just in the nick of time from Hitler's evil men."

The 47th armored infantry were responsible for cleaning the remaining Germans out of the city after the 628th made it through with their tanks. Remaining snipers located in some of the buildings were flushed out by these soldiers and killed as the last remaining element of the German forces were cleared out by the American ground troops.

> "Charles de Gaulle wasn't anywhere around. I never saw him or any of the French Army there while we drove through. We chased the Germans out of Paris, not the French! The 628th liberated that city! We did it and had the Germans on the run and that's the way it happened. I saw on a documentary on television that he paraded through the streets like he was responsible for liberating his people which just isn't true and it always pissed me off that it was told like that. After we left the city, I saw a few French guerilla fighters that waived at us and we just kept on going. No French army and certainly no Charles de Gaulle!"

After turning at the Arc de Triumph, the men of the 628th Tank Destroyer Battalion cautiously moved toward their next goal which was to cross the Rhine River and enter the German motherland. To meet this goal would mean that the Allied Forces were certain of victory. So the men of these units proceeded and were becoming a hardened fighting unit which would be necessary for what they may find as they meet an enemy head on while trying to protect their territory as well as their Furor, Adolph Hitler.

The men stopped for a brief time and found a small bar that was operated by an Italian man who spoke broken English. As an appreciative business owner within the city of Paris, the man offered all the men of the 628th some hot coffee with cognac. The soldiers gladly accepted and were served this treat that was such a nice gesture and helped them to forget about what they were all doing for those fleeting moments. As they were served the coffee by the young daughter of this Italian man, the boys of the 628th noticed her beauty and couldn't help but stare into the face of who seemed to be an angel living and serving them in the middle of what could be called *hell!*

> "The father told us, you can-a-look-a, but you cannot-a-touch-a! We all laughed with him and drank the coffee. It tasted like embalming fluid! It was so strong with the cognac that I really didn't like it but it was nice of them to give us this expensive drink anyhow."

Just outside of Paris, the 628th had some opposition with the Germans and the tanks were taking care of this small skirmish. The other men, including Charles and his passengers, were held up and waiting for the all clear. While waiting, they came across a vineyard which made French champagne. As another gesture to the Americans, the workers started coming out from the building handing the soldiers bottles of this expensive drink. The deep appreciation for their liberation was overwhelming and whatever they could offer to the American GI's was also appreciated by each of these homesick and weary young soldiers.

> "I told them, hey you guys, why don't you hand me a case, and they gave me one! I had six bottles in my vehicle! That made two bottles a piece for us guys on the command vehicle and we were very happy to get it. I saved mine for later and drank it one night after I was off of guard duty. It was the good stuff and I slept really well that night for a change."

As the residents of this village near the Argonne Forest began to file back into the streets, the 628th was greeted by some of the very appreciative French citizens. An old man walking with the aid of crutches approached Charles's command car. He seemed anxious to speak to Charles and motioned for him to look at some items that he was carrying with him.

> "He was standing along my car and he motioned to look at his medals, speaking French to me with some English mixed in. We were in the area where WWI had ended and I saw the remains of several trenches that the French had dug there. I could see old rusted canteens and other personal items that they used back then. He raised one finger and told me that he had won these in WWI and told me that I was 2, meaning WWII. He extended his hand that had two medals in it and said to me, *this is for you.* I took the medals and told him thank you. He nodded and thanked us for coming back to help them once again. He stood there for a while and spoke to several other soldiers in their cars as I pulled away from the touching moment. I kept those medals with me for quite a while in my duffle bag. I had to leave the bag in Bastogne one day in a theater, intending to pick them up again, but the Germans got to our stuff first and ransacked all of our bags and I lost everything I had left there to the damn Germans. I still am very upset that I lost that man's medals. They were beautiful and they meant a lot to me as well as the man that won them."

Mr. Libby also makes note that the men had to dig ditches from time to time to bury garbage and items that may alert the Germans as to where they may have been, what they may have for remaining supplies and possibly know what condition the men were in physically. Although Mr. Libby had never seen a German Sheppard that was used by the German armies to detect the enemy, they all knew that they were used and every precaution was taken when they were in a sensitive German controlled area. This must had rang true to the soldiers in WWI as well who had placed the items that Charles had seen in this ditch that was partially uncovered from the years of erosion and natural wear.

Shortly after the soldiers had left the city of Paris, the 628th was sitting on the side of the road waiting for orders to advance. A Belgian man, his family and many others were walking along the roadside on their way back to Belgium. One particular man spoke English and told a soldier from the tank unit that from the road on their journey, he had seen four German .88 anti-aircraft guns hidden in a large hedgerow and heard that the Germans were going to work the men over the next morning. The 47th Infantry assembled and formulated a plan to send twelve men into the German area and take out these big and very dangerous guns. During the night, the Germans had boxed these American units in to aid in keeping them contained until they were ready to strike the next day. The 47th were careful not to shoot to draw fire and would have to be as silent as possible while slipping through their positions. Mr. Libby recalls that the men split up into four groups of three in each and were each assigned to a German gun. The men advanced forward making their way to the seventh hedgerow where they had found these big guns were located. The German guards were eliminated by the 47th Infantry by the use of their knives to stay undetected. With synchronized watches, the men each dropped a phosphorus grenade into the barrels of each gun, melting them much like ice cubes sitting in the hot sun. Sometime later, the men returned with the all clear status and the American units were able to advance and to avoid the battle that they had planned for them that day without any American casualties and without drawing any enemy gunfire in the darkness of the night.

> "We were sure glad that the Belgian guy we met had told us about those big German guns. They had us boxed in and they would have given us quite a workout if the guys from the 47th hadn't risked their lives and gone in there and destroyed those big guns. Those guys were really tough, we knew that and we really appreciated them being beside us in the fighting!"

The men of the 628th encountered another large German gun along their path as they were moving up a nearby hill. This German .88 fired on the unit and hit one of their tanks blowing out one of its tracks known as a cat. The unit moved off the road and took cover after this lone shot. Fortunately for the Americans, this proved to be the only shot that the Germans took with this big gun. Engineers from the rear echelon quickly moved in to start the repairs to this valuable piece of fighting equipment. Later that night, when the all-clear was given, the unit collectively moved forward and the engineers brought their tank back to them, ready to fire when needed. The unit moved into a strategic position and orders were given to move a tank up the hill to take the German gun out that had caused this damage.

> "A sergeant that was in charge of the tank fell to the ground and started to dig his fingers into the gravel on the side of the road. He was losing his mind! He kept saying over and over that he wasn't going to send another tank up there. He was worried that another tank would get hit or his guys would get killed! He just kept digging his hands into the gravel until all of his fingers were bleeding. Some men came in a jeep and took him to the rear echelon and we never

> saw him again. I guess it all finally got to him and he just cracked. I felt bad for him."

The unit advanced and the 47th Infantry moved in and did the type of job that they were trained for. After approaching the big gun and ready to take out the Germans who manned it, they found that after their lone shot they had all ran away in fear of counter-attacks and left it unattended. For now, no more worries for the tank destroyers, at this particular position.

> "As I was driving by the big gun, I saw a soldier from the 47th take out a white phosphorous grenade and drop it into the barrel of the .88 gun barrel. It just melted in a matter of seconds. That was a really cool thing to watch as its barrel melted just like chocolate in the sun."

Damaged German tank from the handy work of the 47th Armored Infantry.

With so many little homes, villages and dirt roads traveled, some of the actual locations of events seem to run together for Mr. Libby at the age of 97. It was a huge challenge to the men who were fighting to document every movement for those who were in charge of such record keeping responsibilities. So many things happened, time managed to continue but at times seemed as if it stood still. Horrors they witnessed, town after town after town, the faces seemed to all look the same, but the stories all seemed to be similar in some form or fashion.

It was somewhere during this timeline, in an open area on the C-Company's travels that Mr. Libby remembers hearing the sound of 50 caliber fire coming from a vehicle behind him in the convoy. Colonel Cole got on the radio and called back to another radio man and asked if they were getting enemy fire or had seen some Germans from the rear echelon. His tone quickly went from eagerness and concern to fuming anger as Mr. Libby tells this humorous story about the men who were firing this big gun.

```
"When Colonel Cole heard the shooting, he
thought that we were under fire in the rear
echelon. He said to them on the radio, are
you getting enemy fire back there? The ra-
dio man said no but that they were shooting
at deer running through a big field. That
was something that he didn't like at all.
He started to raise his voice and asked them
what they would do if they were engaged by
the enemy and were out of ammunition be-
cause they used it all on shooting at deer.
He was mad as hell! Then he said that he was
going to come back there and do some of his
own shooting if they didn't stop shooting
at deer. Needless to say, they stopped and
we moved forward again to our next location,
```

> and the deer of the area, they were all safe
> from us."

Another ten miles down the road as they units left the area of the wineries, Paris was no longer in their sights. The men of the 628th, with the aid of a bulldozer, backed their tanks into position for artillery fire. The unit set up camp there for three days near this small village. The unit would come under heavy artillery fire and returned fire back toward the Germans several times during this brief stay. It was now obvious that their position had been compromised and in a move to help to secure their further movements and their numbers, the men of the 628th were told by commanders of HQ to evacuate all of the citizens in this small village to flush out the potential spy which was among them. These three days were filled with chores, repairs and other small duties that needed to be attended to after their long trip through France and the many small battles they had encountered along the dangerous path through German occupied territory.

Mr. Libby recalls a time just after the citizens were evacuated when they started to explore the homes to see if there was anything to lead them to finding the spy or any other type of important and helpful information. Some of the soldiers also found it to be a time to loot a little to see what kinds of souvenirs they could possibly ship home to their family that the Germans had stashed there to use against the American troops like pistols, rifles or any other German military items.

> "There were about ten of us that walked into
> a farm house and up the stairs into the
> kitchen. We came across a steaming hot din-
> ner all prepared and on the big wooden din-
> ner table. We all sat down and enjoyed the
> meal that was left behind by the owners. It
> was roast beef, mashed potatoes, corn, beans,
> celery, lettuce, bread and hot coffee. We all
> sat down and ate a good home-cooked meal.

After eating this feast and still sitting at the table, Captain Jones came into the farm house, saw what we had consumed and asked us if we enjoyed the meal. We all said, yeah Captain, it was really good. Captain Jones looked at us and said, "*what if it was poisoned?*" We were speechless and looked at one-another waiting to see if it had indeed been poisoned. Thank God it wasn't! After the meal, we all went upstairs and found some comfortable beds for a rest. I took off my shoes and my helmet and lay down in one of the beds fully clothed with three others who had also climbed in. Another bed held four more of our guys as well to get a much needed rest."

After the speech from Captain Jones, the boys thought a little while about what could had happened to them. In the future, Captain Jones's cautious words rang in the ears of these young inexperienced men. These young soldiers needed to fully understand that the dangers of this war were spread out everywhere! They came in many forms and that if they made the wrong choices, even as simple as sitting down to a hot meal, it could cost them all their lives!

"Captain Jones was always cool. He was just like Clint Eastwood. A cool-headed guy and never got excited about anything. A bullet would fly by us and sometimes he would duck just a little bit and sometimes he wouldn't even duck at all. He just sat there and didn't let it bother him at all. I really liked him."

At around six o'clock the next morning, the men were awoken by a noise that seemed to be a German patrol. As the boys moved their way down the stairs with rifles in hand, they saw what the noises were from. The men from the unit who were left outside that night to stand guard had decided to play a trick on the sleeping 628th soldiers upstairs. They had lured a farmer's cow into the kitchen and the panicked cow on the slippery kitchen floor provided the noise that alerted the boys that something was up. As they made their way downstairs with guns in hand, the cow hit the kitchen table while trying to remain standing sending plates flying into the air and eventually crashing down to the floor. The boys felt very relieved knowing that it wasn't a German patrol in the house, but still wanted to get to the bottom of who orchestrated the harmless prank that disturbed their much needed, short rest.

"I said to the guys outside, you bastards put that heifer in there didn't you? The guys of the 47th all denied it and said that it got in there all on its own. They were all laughing like hell! I said to them, yeah, it just walked in the house looking for something to eat. I went back inside shaking my head. It really scared the heck out of us, but it was all in fun."

Mr. Libby further comments about the wealth of farm animals that he saw during his time there. A treat for the nightly dinner, when it presented itself, a rare opportunity to kill and butcher one when they would bivouac in an area that raised animals was something that the men dreamed of. Anything that could replace the 10-in-1 rations for a meal was certainly worthy of a search for this form of nutrition.

"We killed a cow once, cut the hind quarters off and hung it up in a tree. The guys from the 82nd killed one and couldn't get theirs up "in the tree so I gave them a hand. The next morning you could slice a steak right off and cook it up. It was a very nice treat for all of us guys. We saw chickens flying around and they would roost in a nearby tree. If you wanted chicken for dinner, you just went out, shot one and it fell out of the tree. On several occasions we found pigs as well that made for a nutritious meal for us. It was always nice to be able to have this kind of food instead of the 10-in-1 rations that were provided to us. There weren't too many wild animals around because the artillery fire would always scare them all away, especially when our guys shoot at the local deer!"

Nearby, the Germans were in a valley and from time to time, would start shooting at the area where they were bivouacked. The mail truck managed to get through and deliver news and letters to all of the men while they were there. The boys of this unit were on the move so much that it could be anywhere from two weeks to a month before they would get it delivered. Charles received a letter at this particular drop off and began to read it as he leaned on the side of the weapons carrier which delivered the mail along with the necessary supplies. This particular letter turned out to be a *Dear John* letter from his girl back home in the states. As he read it, a dog fight ensued directly over the camp between the Americans and Germans which began to send bullets ricocheting off the roof of a barn and bright airbursts overhead sent blue, yellow and white colored, hot shrapnel to the ground.

"I loved this girl back home in Pennsylvania and dated her for almost eight years. Earline told me in this letter that she was in love with another man. I was in shock as I read the letter. I was standing out in the open basically and the other guys were yelling at me from inside of the nearby barn. They kept yelling, get in here Libby! They kept telling me that she wasn't worth it. After I snapped out of it and realized what was going on around me, I went inside with them to be better protected from the gun fire and shrapnel. I thought it over for a little while and knew that I had work to do and dropped it from my mind because I had more important things to think about and I'd deal with it someday when I finally got home. I had a job to do and it came first above anything else, even girls."

During their stay here in this particular village, many soldiers would come back from the closer battles and skirmishes that ensued around the area. The soldiers all gathered in a barn which was located near their staging area and would rest, talk and write letters to loved ones back home. Injured soldiers would also be brought there to get out of the elements to be taken care of before the ambulance would ultimately take them to another area where they would get a more advanced treatment for their particular injuries. On the day they were all getting ready to pull out and advance when an injured lieutenant was brought into the barn with a serious shrapnel injury to his arm. According to Mr. Libby, it was very bloody and quite a sight to see. The injury caused the unit medic to get sick to his stomach and leave the barn for a moment to get some fresh air. Another lieutenant who was aiding in the medical emergency asked Charles to hold the soldier's arm up so that he could try to bandage the open wound. Charles agreed and did it without any type of hesitation or sickness.

"The lieutenant that asked me to help said, look here and reached his hand to his own head and lifted his skull up that had been cracked open and I could actually see his brain. Nothing was damaged inside, but his skull wasn't attached all the way and you could open it up like a tea pot. He asked me why I wasn't a medic. He told me if that didn't bother me that I should have been one. Then he told me if I wanted to be one, he'd talk to the unit and get me transferred over. I told him no sir, I'm in a tank outfit and I'll stay there, but thank you anyway."

After this three day period of waiting for commands to advance, the men were loaded up and ready to make their way into the country of Belgium. Luxembourg would be their next major goal with many little skirmishes and German snipers along the dangerous path. Slow movements and carefully planned decisions along the way to keep all the men safe was the concern of each commander. Charles would drive along ever wary of his surroundings, carefully listening to the commands that were passed down from the front lines as his radio man Peterson told them to Captain Jones.

Languages were not taught to all of these enlisted men, but Charles took it upon himself to learn valuable sayings and commands to shout at prisoners just by listening to the locals of each country, which also proved to be a valuable tool many times over. Still remembering many of these important sayings, Mr. Libby recites them to me as if he was saying them directly to a German soldier or asking the French residents for many necessary items. He comments that you had to be smart and learn whatever you could to survive during these times. It also proved to be valuable to your superiors in times of need. If information was being gathered from the enemy, to have the knowledge of some of the sayings from their language would aid in the long and arduous process of interrogation.

> "Near Belgium, I found many citizens that knew English because they had to learn it in school as a regular class. I spoke to a married couple one day on a road that spoke English as well as I did. They told us that we could go into their church and look around if we liked. We said thank you and moved on but it was nice to find good speaking people that understood what I was asking them."

Along this path to Luxembourg, Charles and Bik were looking near some houses for a chicken coup to find some eggs for breakfast. Charles looked up toward the yard and saw a little girl walking in the snow without any shoes. Charles immediately picked her up and carried her to his vehicle and sat her on the plate iron. Once again, the languages that Charles had started to pick up came in handy in communicating with the little girl. Previously in Paris, a train box car had been blown out which was carrying many different items. Among these items were womens under clothing and shoes of all sizes. In the event that the soldiers would need to trade something for food or necessary supplies, Charles knew ahead of time to grab what he could from this now disabled box car and keep it handy in the event of a supply shortage. Instead of a trading this item, they now would be a gift that Mr. Libby himself believes that God allowed him to find for that little girl in need. Telling the story with a slight crack in his voice and a tear in his eye, he said this about the little girl . . .

> "I went through all the shoes that I had with me to find a pair that would fit her. First I took a pair of GI socks and placed them on her feet. I folded the ends over so that they would fit the little girl who was only about four years old. I tried a pair

> of shoes on her and they fit just right with the socks on. She kissed me on the cheek and ran home. The next day as we were pulling out, she waived at me when she noticed my vehicle. I guess she recognized the painting on the fender. She then pointed and told her mother who was standing beside her something and she started to waive and smiled at me as if to say thank you. I reached up through the vehicle and waived back to let her know that I saw her. That was the last time that I ever saw that precious little girl, but I can still remember that cute little face and enjoy telling that story very much."

As the 628th moved onward, the citizens of Luxembourg were very pleased to see the American forces roll through their towns with their tanks and soldiers. Not much fighting in this area but as Mr. Libby stated, they had to be watchful of deadly land mines that the Germans had planted there before their arrival and equally aware of the possibility of hidden German snipers.

> "The people were good to us and we got a lot done there during our brief stay. They weren't afraid of us after having the Germans there. We had a lot of cleaning; greasing and basic maintenance to do while we were there before moving on and we had to get it done quickly because we always moved so fast. This area also had trains that would run equipment and supplies to us when we needed them. This was a big help to us especially when we needed gas for the

```
tanks and other vehicles. Railroads also
played an important part in the war for
our units."
```

The 628th had some railroad guns set up in this area that they fired toward the Germans. These guns were named railroad guns due to their size being much like a large train car. Mr. Libby remembers seeing these large guns and hearing them as they were fired at the enemy.

```
"They would raise the shingles right off of
a house when we fired them! They were so big
that you could see them a long ways away.
They fired a huge projectile into the air
that you could see come out of the barrel!
What a sight to see and hear."
```

Mr. Libby remembers the *dragon's teeth* anti-tank obstacles and the barbed wire traps that the Germans used among their belt of items to stop them near Wallendorf. Pill boxes and plenty of mines were obstacles he was watching for from his command car on a regular basis. All of these techniques used by the Germans were certainly irritating to the Americans, but not without ways to overcome these obstacles. Attached to the 628th was a highly trained group of men who were engineers. These men were attached to the unit with one mission along the way through Europe, to fix what was broken. These men were to solve the biggest of problems that would save time and ultimately save the lives of American soldiers.

```
"They threw everything at us in this area!
We were fighting just as hard but got pushed
back. All of the obstacles and all of the
artillery was quite a challenge for us. It
was time for the engineers to step up and
do their job faster than ever."
```

These sections of concrete were strategically placed to disrupt the movements of the American military's vehicles as well as the much feared tanks. The problem was an easy fix for these engineers that amazingly took little time to plan the solution and to properly execute it. Mr. Libby tells about this time interrupted by laughter as he remembers the mistake of the Germans.

> "The Germans didn't make them high enough! The engineers just took our bulldozers and moved stone and gravel near them to have a foundation and then they pushed dirt around them and built it up enough that we just drove right over top of them. As smart as the Germans were, we couldn't believe that they didn't think to make them a little bigger. So much for the dragon's teeth."

Liberation of this area by the 628th was appreciated long after the soldiers went back home to their families in the United States. At a 628th reunion, Mr. Libby remarked that a soldier had traveled back to that same area and that the government there had erected a monument to pay tribute to their unit for their many sacrifices.

> "I really would love to go back there now and see that. They were really nice to us and we were glad to help them. I'm sure it looks really different now without the signs of war that I saw in the 1940's."

Like many of the stopping points along the bloody path of the 628th, the boys of this tank unit actually have little time to think. Thinking is not always a good thing with a soldier that is recapping the battle that he just fought or the horror that he had just witnessed. Along another dirt road, which looked much like many of the others Charles drove, there was a barn which also looked much like the others that they had all slept in along the journey. A fellow C- Company soldier had finally reached his limits to what he saw, heard, smelled and lived. This half-track radio operator had seen all that he could handle and wanted no part of the war, his unit or anything to do with what was happening to him at the time. Several GI's were talking between themselves about the situation, overheard by Charles, the details of his mental condition caused concern for his brother-in-arms.

> "He was getting almost radical and uncontrollable with the other GI's that were trying to talk sense into the distraught soldier. They didn't want anything to do with him because he wasn't allowing anyone to get near him or to talk to him who were trying to help him out."

Charles took it upon himself to go into the barn and try to talk some form of sense into this ailing soldier. One concern of Charles was that he probably hadn't had anything to eat in several days. As he opened the barn door and entered, Charles found the distraught soldier huddled up in a dark corner all by himself. Charles approached the man and tried to start some basic conversation.

> "He looked at me with a look like he was out in some kind of space orbit. I told him that I just wanted to talk to him and he told me to get away and to leave him alone. I told him that he *was* going to talk to me and asked him if he had anything to eat. I wasn't scared of him and I wasn't going to let him try to bully me like he had done to the other GI's. He told me that he hadn't had anything to eat for about three days so I told him that I was going to go out

> to my command car and get him some coffee and some corned beef hash. I also told him that if he didn't eat it that he *was* going to wear it! I turned around and started back out to my car to help this guy that everyone else had all but given up on."

At this very same time, German mortar fire had started to come into parts of this village. Charles was warned by the other soldiers who were taking refuge within the barn to be very careful because it was starting to get hot out there. Some of the GI's even told Libby that he was crazy for going out there for this guy that didn't want anyone's help and risk his own life just to get him something to eat. But to Charles, he felt that this boy was his friend and he needed the help of someone that cared and would want someone to do the same for him if he had ever gotten to this point during the war.

> "Any of them, including myself, would have wanted someone to help them if it happened to them. You never knew when you could break in those conditions. I knew I had to help this guy."

So, as he made his way out to the command car to prepare the meal for this soldier, Charles heard the feared sound of the German mortar shells being fired on the area. To Charles's good fortune, the shells were landing far beyond the road which they were parked on. Ducking behind a tank first and then a half-track that was near his command car, they gave him the cover he needed in the event that the rounds started hitting closer than the last. Finally he made it to the command car to get what he felt the soldier needed so desperately.

The meal was prepared and it was now time to deliver this comfort food to the distraught soldier. Making his way back into the barn wasn't easy by any means as another barrage of shells was fired on this area. Again, bad intelligence and poor firing coordinates by the Germans helped young Charles to safely reach the old barn unscathed with his comforting payload intended for the fellow soldier in need. Looking a little more comfortable when seeing the food and the coffee, the GI settled down considerably. He proceeded to eat the food and Charles sat near him to make sure that he got this much needed nutrition into his body. A hard tack oatmeal cookie for desert and the friendly and comforting words from Charles helped to defuse a potentially dangerous situation for everyone within the tired and hurting unit of fighters.

"The situation could have been very serious and I told Captain Jones that he could upset some of the other guys. Captain Jones said to me that if the mail truck came through later that he would send him back to a medical unit to get him some help. Later that day, when the truck came into the temporary camp, I told the driver that Captain Jones had told me to help load him into the truck to take him back at HQ. The driver told him that he could use him at HQ because he was a radio man and that they needed one in the unit. This really relaxed him and it also helped the ego of this suffering soldier. We were all very glad that it ended without any further incident."

Later, Captain Jones asked if the soldier had been sent to HQ and Charles told him the story that the GI from HQ had told this suffering soldier. Captain Jones seemed to be happy with the results and gave a smile to the young Charles who had handled this situation with a smart combination of discipline and Christian human compassion.

A village in Belgium added some work to C-Company and for Charles himself. Along the road traveling through this particular city, a German soldier ran away from the approaching unit and made his way into an open cellar way. After making his way down the steps, the unit got within striking distance.

> "We were moving quickly and when we got to him, he was trying to open the door at the bottom of the steps leading into this house's cellar. I took a grenade out of the box that we kept in the command car behind the front seat and when we got to the cellar way, I pulled the pin and tossed it down there and kept on driving. We heard it go off about three seconds later and I just kept on driving. We all figured since he wasn't all the way in the house that he got killed. This was only time I got to throw a hand grenade in combat and I guess this is my one and only German kill in the war, but I didn't want to go back to see for sure. Nobody can survive those grenades blasts from such a close distance. I felt bad, but I had a job to do and he really wanted to kill all of us."

After they cleared the city and had settled down for rest and chow, it was time for the dreaded chore of burying the unit's garbage and other items that the Americans didn't want the Germans to find. Dyda was chosen for the detail to have the shallow hole dug before they pulled out. He grabbed two POW's that they had just taken nearby. These prisoners were Polish in nationality and were used as soldiers by the Germans to fight for them.

"I drove by Dyda and asked him what they were doing. He told me that he had these Polish guys that they captured and he told them to dig the hole to bury the garbage. I smiled at him and told him to tell them in Polish that they were digging their own grave and then I drove off laughing. A little while later I came back by and they were still digging the same hole. I asked Dyda why it wasn't done and he yelled back at me that when he told them what I said they both slowed down to a crawl! I laughed and kept going where I needed to go. I guess they weren't in too big a hurry to dig what they thought was their own grave."

Moving toward the city of Bastogne, the 47th armored infantry was ahead of the 628th Tank Destroyer Battalion and both were moving in high gear! They were instructed that stops were to be minimal and when they did stop, they were to take care of their personal business quickly and get right back into their vehicles to be ready to pull out once again!

"We drove a day, a night and another entire day to get there. Late on the third day we got there and the 82nd Airborne had already made a drop the night before so we weren't alone. We followed Patton all the way there and he wasn't taking his time. We had to get over there and quickly! He had told the European command that he'd get there in three days and we all did it."

Along this path, a soldier found a 45 caliber pistol lying in the middle of the road. As he made a comment that he had found a beautiful pistol, another soldier yelled to him not to touch it or he would get blown to pieces and to quickly step back away from this German booby trap.

> "The one soldier along with us knew about bombs and what to do when he found them. He tied some black thread he had in his ruck sack around the trigger guard after digging the dirt out around it. He was careful not to move the gun because he knew that it was booby-trapped by the Germans and one wrong move could do him in. He slowly moved off of the road allowing the thread to unwind from his hand as he got farther away and when he was fair enough distance away from the pistol, he got down on the ground and then pulled the thread. The booby trap went off and destroyed that beautiful gun and blew dirt everywhere. It wasn't too powerful, but powerful enough to kill or seriously injure any American soldier reaching down to pick up a souvenir to take home with them. Those Germans had all kinds of booby-traps that we had to watch out for all the time. That soldier was very lucky that someone knew about those traps and stopped him that day."

Near the city, the men of C-Company found a dead German soldier lying face down in a ditch on the side of the road. A routine check of the body ensued for information and to see if the soldier was actually dead. After the quick inspection, some of the men decided that it would be funny to prop the soldier up in the ditch at attention to get a rise out of the other men driving by.

> "We would drive by him on our duties and jokingly salute him and say, morning Fritz. It got to where the other companies were doing it as well after seeing us do it. You had to do stuff like that for moral and to make light of some of the stuff that we were seeing and doing. But, for every dead German that we saw, we'd see a dead American that would stop us in our tracks and would get us thinking, if I'm not careful, that could be me laying there."

Bastogne, Belgium proved to the US forces that they really had the German forces on the run. As they moved deeper into German occupied territory, it became apparent that the US forces were definitely gaining ground. Now approaching the heart of the city, the Americans came into a pinch point on the now famous Autobahn Highway which placed them only meters away from the German forces. Surrounding the Germans in a grassy area between the roads where it became a "Y", American forces came across two 88's and a large contingency of German soldiers who were unaware that it was American troops that were closing in on them. Radio silence at this point was a must and any type of communications that would give the enemy any advantage. According to Mr. Libby, the Americans weren't too sure that it was even Germans that they themselves were approaching.

> "You see, in this area we were in, it was hard to tell who was there. The Germans thought we were Germans and we thought the Germans were Americans at first. When we finally realized that it was Germans, we had to quickly access the situation and get into a strategic position to fight. The problem was that if we shot toward them, we

could hit the other Americans that were on the other road which connected to where we were. The 109th Infantry got up on a hill and moved down into the grassy area and started to do their thing taking out the nearest group of German soldiers first. The Germans were shooting with their rifles in every direction after they realized that it was Americans that were right on top of them. Then, our guys took two phosphorous grenades and dropped them down into their big guns. It melted the barrels just like melting ice over a flame. Every time I saw that, I was amazed at how fast they destroyed that thick metal of the gun."

Mr. Libby makes further statements about this particular area itself with strong memories which still ring loudly in his ears and clearly run through his mind by saying this...

"That was a pretty hot battle and there was shooting all over the place. We were basically stuck there and had to fight hard to take these guys out! We could hear our other guys fighting near us as well chasing Germans back into Germany. This is why we had to stay on that particular part of the hill. The battle going on above us was too hot to move into and then on top of that, we were stuck there. There was shooting all over the place from rifles, tanks and anti-aircraft fire. This was everything that you

> hear a battle was like and it was really loud!"

While waiting on the hilltop for orders to move up farther into the main battle, the 628th stood posed, anxious to be able to contribute their manpower to their brothers-in-arms. This marks the only place that Charles had the rare opportunities to actually get a glimpse and see the one and only General George S. Patton in action on the battlefield. From a distance, Charles saw the general get out of a jeep, walk around with an officer and then get back into his vehicle and pull away.

> "I knew it was him from a distance and was surprised that he had come back that far. He was always right up at the front in the action. I recognized his uniform and the way that he was being respected and listened to by the men around him. I didn't get a chance to go and speak to him but was glad that I got to see him. We all liked him very much and were very proud to be under his command."

Shortly after this, a Sherman tank approached Charles's command car that had just came back from the rear echelon in the ordinance area. This tank from the 3rd Armored Division was manned by a Tech Sgt. Driver, a 1st Lieutenant and another Sergeant. Libby and the boys in the area met the tank driver along the roadside and went over to give them an important message about what they may find ahead. The report was that there were some German soldiers still hiding in a thick hedgerow near an old farmhouse ahead to the left of the actual tank battle that was still going hot and heavy. Mr. Libby recalls the important instructions they told these soldiers and tells it as if it was yesterday.

"The three GI's came back from ordinance and we told them that there was still some Germans up there in the hedgerow. They were full of piss and vinegar and were sort of smug with us. Captain Jones told them to be very careful and spray it good with machine gun fire to get them out of there before we would have to pass through. About fifteen minutes later we heard the loud blast of a bazooka. We knew right away that those sons-of-bitches hit that tank! It was only a few minutes later that the tank driver came back toward us in the crippled tank and crying."

The distraught tank driver was sobbing and told the men of the 628th that the Germans had hit his tank with a bazooka shell and that his boys were both dead! After the tank driver described what had just happened, Captain Jones asked Charles to aid in the removal of the two bodies. He also asked Peterson to radio for an ambulance to take the bodies back to the rear echelon and be properly taken care of. At that point Captain Jones asked the tank driver if he wanted him to contact his unit to tell them what happened. Captain Jones personally took the radio and contacted the proper units to tell of this terrible misfortune which befell the two American soldiers.

"I climbed up on the tank and looked down into the space and saw that the two soldiers were lying there dead, at least what was left of them. I had to reach down in there and both of my arms immediately got covered with blood. I started to pull the first soldier out by grabbing under his arms but had to stop for a moment to slide his head back over into the correct position. His face was

```
gone and I was trying to make sure that I
had his whole body when I pulled him out of
the tank. When I lifted the second soldier
out, we had to slide his head over as well
that was almost cut all the way off from the
shrapnel. For several days, that was all I
could think about. It was terrible!"
```

When the sad chore of loading the dead into an ambulance was finished, Captain Jones showed the most emotion to that point that Charles had seen from him and told young Charles in a stern manner to get into the command car. Not only Charles loaded up to go after the Germans, but several of the men of the 47th Armored Infantry climbed on top of the vehicle to go and aid in this mission to hunt down these murderers.

```
"He told me to get in the vehicle and let's
go get those bastards! The 47th guys were
hanging all over my vehicle. They knew where
we were going and they wanted to help to
take them out. Captain Jones didn't say much
but I could tell by his expression that he
really meant business."
```

As Charles reached the area, instead of driving along the side of the hedgerow, he used quick thinking and capitalized on his own sadness and anger by driving straight into the heavy brush to flush them out. When they heard the large vehicle coming straight toward them, four German soldiers fled the thick hedgerow with their hands held up high in the air yelling,

"*Comrade, Comrade!*" All of the men of the 47th Armored Infantry who had climbed onto the command car immediately jumped off of and took the four Germans as prisoners or war. Captain Jones exited the vehicle and spoke to another vehicle driver who had approached after seeing the commotion in the hedgerow. The 47th Infantry began their tough interrogation with the men and made it short, sweet and to the point . . .

"I was watching all of them from my vehicle. They were near a farmhouse now standing with their hands up in the air. I could hear one of the soldiers who was talking to them start yelling, *you guys only surrender when you're out of bazooka shells*. At that point, in one smooth motion, the soldier fired in a straight line once to the right and once to the left with automatic fire across the bodies of the German soldiers, killing them where they stood! When they were dead, the guys searched their bodies to find anything that would give us information about the other German troops in the area."

Captain Jones knew that the anger of these men was high and that what they did to these soldiers was a justified move and without time to take prisoners during a heated battle which was going on just a few miles from this particular situation, he turned a blind eye and the men went back to their staging area until it was safe enough for all of them to move forward into the city of Bastogne.

"Captain Jones had gone over to the bodies himself and took a pistol from one of the dead soldiers. He walked toward the vehicle and yelled to me, *here Libby* and threw me a Lugar in its hard leather case. I still have it today and consider it one of my prized possessions. I guess that Captain Jones thought the way I drove into the hedgerow without any fear was a good move that led

> us to finding those German soldiers. As we were getting ready to leave, one of the 47th guys climbed back onto the vehicle and said to me, *now, they are good German soldiers.*"

Sergeant Erdos was a half-track driver in C-Company and a friend of Charles. During this particular time in the movement of the units, the weather was very bad. Cold was not the word that Mr. Libby would describe it, as if there was an even stronger word that came into his mind for the frigid temperatures they were enduring. The men were certainly suffering physically from the extreme weather conditions and some of the drivers and ground troops that had more exposure to the elements than others were feeling it's harmful effects.

> "A few of the men had to lift him out of his half-track and get him to a medical tent in the rear echelon quickly! His feet and his legs had actually frozen solid. He knew that he had to stay in his vehicle and that he couldn't get out and walk around to get the blood flowing. I felt really badly about it. I liked him very much and we were pretty good friends. After they carefully lifted him out of the vehicle, I was standing there close to him. He looked at me and said, *well Charlie, I hope I see you again.* I looked back at him and said I hope so buddy. They loaded him up and drove him away to get some help. I never saw him again, not even at the reunions years later."

This is just one of the men that suffered from the weather that certainly affected troop movements and the outcome of several battles. The equipment would suffer as well along the way during these months and the roads would become impassable at times until the units could get areas plowed for the tanks and other vehicles to move through. Mother Nature didn't care about a war going on and the spring months were certainly welcomed by many when they finally came along. Traveling and fighting each battle were both seriously affected by the seasonal weather patterns.

As the 628th C-company reached Bastogne, the men helped out for a short time to remove dead American bodies and load injured American soldiers into the several ambulances that were now in the area. The men of the 82nd Airborne were waiting there for trucks to come and pick them up as well now that their dangerous work was finished in that area.

```
"When things started to settle down, the
guys of the 82nd were walking down the road
and I asked them where they were going. One
of the guys looked at me and said that they
were going to see if they could find some
Krauts. He told me not to worry that they'd
be back sometime tomorrow. I asked the one
where his rifle was and he said to me, when
he gets shot, pointing at his buddy, I'll
use his. Crazy bastard! The next day, they
were coming up the road in two brand new
German half-track vehicles. We thought it
was Germans at first and then one of our
buck sergeants yelled, don't shoot! They have
American helmets on, it's our guys. I told
them that they almost got their asses shot
off and they just laughed and said to me, we
knew that you guys would recognize us."
```

At 0400 the next morning, the men of the 82nd Airborne were picked up and moved by trucks to their next assignment deep in the heart of German territory.

Much like the 628th, the 82nd kept moving along quickly, but their specialty was jumping into enemy territory on a daily basis unlike the 628th that always stayed on the ground.

> "When they left, they took all of our pots and pans that we cooked in. We bitched for a while and then we had to go and steal more for ourselves to have something to cook in. They didn't just take ours; they took a bunch from A and B Company as well. I was just glad that they didn't take our stove. I'll tell you, those guys were really something else."

The 628th continued to move through small villages along the way before moving into the bigger towns and major cities which produced several battles that they faced with bravery and at times, a little luck and most certainly, a blessing from above.

> "Most of the cities didn't even have any markers or signs to identify them so I really can't remember all the small ones that I was in or drove through. Hell, the Germans would even change or move the signs to throw us off! Good thing we had a lot of map problems during our American maneuvers or we would had been in serious trouble many times."

Aberfontain, Belgium was surrounded by the incoming American forces. The 628th was part of this plan due to the intelligence that the city held German foot soldiers. This particular unit had light weapons which included bazookas and machine guns. The 628th hit the city hard with tank fire and the 47th Infantry moved in to fully secure the once occupied city.

The after-effects of a shell fired by one of the US M-36 Tanks.

"Germans hid in anything they could to try to go undetected. We took several Germans prisoners in this city. I was watching the Germans march past us into the trucks that we had there to take them to the rear echelon. As one of the soldiers was passing, I noticed something he had on that nobody else had noticed. I pointed to the Kraut soldier and one of the lieutenants and a captain asked me what I was pointing at. I said, sir, do you see what that German has on? He got pissed and said, *No! What is it that you see and I don't see soldier?* I told him that he was wearing a pair of GI shoes and that he either killed a GI to get them or took them off of a dead American soldier's body. He told one of the line sergeants to pull

> that German out of the group and to sit down in the snow and take the shoes off before he was loaded into the prisoner truck. The two officers just walked away after that and I continued to watch the line looking for anything else that I could find to be helpful."

German pill boxes or bunkers were found scattered all over the landscape. Most were blown out previously before the 628th found them. One particular day on the path to Mannheim, Germany, the men approached one of these pill boxes on a high cliff that wasn't blown out yet. As the entire convoy was rolling by and a German soldier opened the door of this fortified bunker and yelled out at the Americans.

> "He yelled at us in German to put our hands up and surrender. He didn't even have a gun; he just stood there yelling at us in German like a complete fool. We were all laughing at him and he went back into the bunker and slammed the door. One of our tank sergeants spun the turret around toward the pill box and fired a 90mm shell right into the door. He wasn't even authorized to do it, he just did it! I heard one of the soldiers say after the shot, *what's in there?* The gunner told him, *a dead German, but you won't be able to find him now.*"

After the unit found a strategic place in a wooded area near Mannheim to set up camp and take care of some maintenance and other necessary chores, the men stretched their legs and began to move about freely among one another on this desolate road. Unknown at the time to the men of the 628th, a small mechanized

German unit was not too far away from these men and their scouts reported to their officer that there was an American unit not too far away on the road near this forest area.

> "Our speculation afterward was that this German unit was tired of the fighting. They were about fifty strong and still had plenty of ammunition to fight if they really wanted to."

Apparently with the command of the German officer to his men, they marched onto the road slowly with a white flag attached to a stick waiving it in the air. This attempt to surrender to the Americans was noticed by the men, especially by a 2nd Lieutenant that was the high ranking officer at the time in that vicinity.

> "The Germans told us that they wanted to surrender and appeared to be very weary and ready to give up. This cocky and obviously inexperienced 2nd Lieutenant told everyone that it was a trick and not to listen to them. He and a few others started to fire on the Germans of this mechanized unit on his command and then all hell broke out! The Germans hesitated to fire back at first because they were sincere about their surrender. They really did want to give up."

Charles and some of the others got down into a ditch to take cover. They all realized that the Germans wanted to surrender and were merely firing back out of self-defense to the actions of this 2nd Lieutenant. After about a half an hour of fighting, many of the GI's discontinued their shooting after seeing that they were still trying to surrender to the American unit by waiving their hands in the air and trying desperately to vocally communicate to the officer. Many of them moved back onto the road waving their arms trying to get the attention of the commander. All shooting came to a halt and the sergeants of the unit wondered why the officer even gave them the command to fire on the Germans. The 2nd Lieutenant was dumfounded at the behavior of the Germans and the reality of this horrible situation finally started to sink into his mind and the look of fear took over his face as he began to realize his fatal mistake with his order to fire on them.

Twenty seven American GI's were killed in that half hour and many more Germans died as well. The officers at HQ were alerted to the situation after hearing the fighting. Officials came to area where the fighting had just occurred and took the 2nd Lieutenant along with the sergeants, who had just witnessed the events for questioning. The men of the unit began the sad and all too familiar chore of cleaning up the dead American bodies to be taken to the rear echelon and processed for their early trip home to the United States. Several men from the rear echelon were also responsible to sift through the German weapons and gear to properly dispose of it or to take it for themselves to use against the Germans if needed.

```
"I can still remember seeing that German
walking down that road wanting to surren-
der. A lot of Americans died for no reason
that day! After they took the prisoners to
the POW Camp and the 2nd Lieutenant was taken
away, we all had a lot of work there to put
the pieces back together and clean every-
thing up. We never saw that officer again.
I've always wondered what happened to him.
I would imagine that he was court-marshaled
for his deadly order he gave."
```

Just as the men were ready to move on and get to their next location, they heard what sounded like the sound of a motor boat in the air. The men knew that the sound was that of a German V-1 bomb. When the V-1 approached the men of the unit they knew just what to do. As they watched the rocket, the men stood still and prepared for the heat wave that comes off of the rocket's engine. Another important thing for the men to do was to open their mouths to prevent their ear drums from popping. The closer it got to the men, the slower the engine started to sound to all of them.

> ```
> "We were watching it get closer after we
> heard it and then the fire coming off of the
> back V-1 went out. When that happens, you
> know that it's going to come down somewhere
> very soon. Fortunately for us, it landed a
> ways a way into the thick forest. It made a
> hell of a noise and blew up a bunch of trees!
> Thank God it landed somewhere else and not
> near us. We were all just recovering from
> the battle that just happened a short time
> ago and were caught completely off guard
> when this thing started toward us."
> ```

It occurred to me when writing this manuscript that Mr. Libby had spent a couple of Christmas days in Europe. I wondered about Mr. Libby and all of the other American soldiers and their feelings of being away from family and their homes on this most special of religious holidays. As soldiers continue to spend this day away from family in the wars of today, Mr. Libby tells his feelings to give them encouragement and to help comfort our soldiers while they all serve.

> ```
> "The first thoughts in my mind were if I was
> going to be home next Christmas. But, af-
> ter you are in there a while, your thoughts
> were doing your job to drive the Germans
> back into the area that we were trying to
> get them back into. I knew that my family
> ```

> was alright back at home and I got a letter from my mother whom said that she hoped I was safe wherever I was and to be home soon. She also said that you boys over there are doing a wonderful thing. That was my Christmas gift that year."

To Charles, this was a wonderful Christmas gift from his caring family. The younger soldiers in the unit were often found crying as they wondered if they would also be home for Christmas the next year. The units bonded even more during this holiday and gave comfort to one-another as they all shared the same home-sick feelings of missing their loving families.

Charles remembers a Christmas story which occurred around Mannheim, Germany. His memory is that the unit was staged at a blown out building without any roof. All four walls were still standing, so it seemed a perfect place to hide and to bed down for the night. As the boys laid down and covered themselves in their sleeping bags, Mr. Libby remembers looking up to the clear winter night sky.

> "I looked up and the stars were bright and the sky was clear as could be. What a beautiful night it was. The Germans must have respected The Lord Jesus that Christmas Eve because no shells were fired on us the entire night and didn't start until the next day. I remember one of the guys saying that they can't all be bad because they allowed us to have a beautiful and quiet night. When I woke up, I was covered in at least three inches of soft white snow. I slept so sound on that beautiful night that I didn't even know that it was snowing. Nothing bothered

us that night and we all got some much needed rest that Christmas Eve."

As the Germans took a posture of retreating, Mr. Libby seems to remember that they threw anything at them that they had remaining in their arsenal to try to cripple the advance of the American forces. The wide-spread use of the V-1 and V-2 bombs by the German army presented a dangerous problem for the men of the 628th. These large bombs had the ability to travel longer distances than any of their artillery and were quite larger carrying a bigger *bang* for their buck.

"They told us how to tell between the two German buzz bombs. The V-1 went straight across the landscape horizontally and the V-2 went straight up into the air and then when it got to its height, it would turn and start to slowly come down at an angle. If you saw the fire coming out of the back, you knew that it would go past you but if you saw the fire go out, you better get somewhere else! They taught us to stand still as they passed us and to open our mouths wide. If you kept your mouth closed, your ear drums would pop. When they exploded they produced a big heat wave that would really rock your entire body. One just missed us in a forest one time and blew a bunch of trees up. We'd scatter if we saw them because they were so powerful!"

When C-Company was ready to leave the Mannheim area the next day, more shelling began to come near the 628th from the Germans. As they started to shell in an attempt to hit the road that the American troops were on, Captain Jones came up with a plan to get his entire company out of there safely.

"I was the lead car and Captain Jones said to me, Libby you go first. If they hear your vehicle, they will certainly hear the louder tanks. So, I went up the road and down through the ravine and gradually up the hill to the stopping point that Captain Jones had identified as the meeting point. He had noticed that there was a space of time between the artillery fire and knew how long it was taking for them to reload their guns. He'd allow them to fire and when it would stop, he would send another piece of equipment. Pretty smart of the captain we all thought."

Sergeant Luckey went after Charles's command car making it safely in his half-track and also safely made it to the designated meeting spot and a jeep quickly followed him. One by one, the tanks rolled up the road safely but not without a couple of close calls along the way. After the shelling had stopped, two or three tanks at a time were able to move safely along the road and eventually up the hill to the meeting spot for the entire C-company.

"Captain Jones waited until everyone had made it there safely before he came up in a jeep. We all made it up there safely and it was because of Captain Jones being smart enough to know how to get us all up that hill that morning."

Another part of this path leading to the Hurtgen Forest was a dirt road which separated planted wheat fields on one side and rough terrain and forest on the opposite side. As they approached the Hurtgen Forest, the men of C-Company noticed several cultivated wheat stalks stacked in large piles in the field to their left hand side. Charles and one other soldier, who was riding with him at the time learning the trade of becoming an orderly, decided to take on a new role to help out the infantry and leave the safety of their vehicle and help to inspect each of these wheat bushels to see if there were Germans hiding behind or underneath any of them. A few other soldiers joined in the search as well which proved to uncover three dead uniformed German soldiers.

> "The 47th had already used flamethrowers there on the field and burned many of the stalks. We went to one particular wheat stock that wasn't burned and there was a dead German sitting there with his eyes opened much like he was ready to attack us. I reached for my pistol thinking that he was still alive. He scared the shit out of me and I almost shot him! The other guy with me lifted his helmet and hat that he was wearing and found a small pistol underneath. He asked me if I wanted it and I told him, no you can have it, I already have one. After we searched the entire area finding only dead Germans, we all loaded back up and continued to move on."

This dirt road had its hazards as well. At one point, Charles had to watch carefully for the German planted road mines. The evidence was right in front of him as he came upon a section of the road where someone had previously set one off by carelessly running over it. Caution was at its highest from this point on. The Command Car itself was strategically lined with sandbags to lessen the effect of running over one of these dangerous and deadly hidden road mines.

The US Army had at their disposal bulldozers that had the specific job of sweeping for land and road mines. Attached to the front of these large pieces of equipment were flapping-types of devices that would actually slap the ground ahead of the main section of the dozer, setting off the dangerous road mines or land and shoe mines found in fields. This procedure saved countless lives for the 47th Armored Infantry. Crossing land to infiltrate the enemy, the many vehicles that traveled the roads and anywhere else that the Germans had found to plant these killers this was a much more primitive form of mine detection than we have at our disposal today, but the soldiers who served then certainly appreciated the men that operated these large pieces of equipment out in front of them.

Looking ahead, the men of the 628th saw the trees of the thick and mysterious looking Hurtgen Forest. The men having previous experience, they realized that every tree could hide a German sniper. Every dark area could hide a soldier with a bazooka or a German tank ready to fire a shell at them. Trees at different points covered the roads much like a tunnel which made it darker and more difficult to maneuver on the treacherous road as well as identifying the outline of a German soldier's body as he waited to shoot at the passing American soldiers and vehicles.

German planes strafed the road and nearby areas the entire time the 628th and other American forces advanced toward the Hurtgen Forest. The problem with this was the speed they were forced to travel as they were wary of the road mines. Charles Libby was lead vehicle once again for the 628th and it was his job to maneuver the command car properly on the road to establish the path that the others would travel coming up behind him. Captain Jones had moved into a smaller jeep with another soldier that was fluent with the German language, but was not too far behind Charles in the event he would need to get into a more secure vehicle or to use the radio which was onboard the armored command car.

```
"The Germans wanted that territory and
didn't want to give it up! They knew how im-
portant it was and how well they were able
to conceal themselves and their operations
```

> within this dense forest. They had every kind of plane they could fly going over us and firing all over the place. We were returning fire when we could see them above the tree lines. We lost some good men on this road and knew the deeper we got into the forest; the worse it was going to be. Sometimes the heavy artillery fire would knock these big trees to the ground and we'd have to watch out for that type of danger as well and take cover. We had to worry more about the mortar fire because you couldn't hear them quite as well or just where it was coming from."

And so, the 628th advanced and continued to fight along the way and took part in what is now known as the *Battle of the Hurtgen Forest*. The unit drove more to the far sides of the road and off of the actual tire tracks to avoid any of these deadly road mines. The infantry had an even tougher time of it with the shoe mines and *bouncing Betty's* which the Germans had placed in the high grassy areas along the roadway. Shoe mines took off many legs and the bouncing Betty's, which were filled with ball bearings, blew in a horizontal manner which would take out much more than a leg. Trip wires that were strung across the roads were another big concern for the many drivers of the smaller vehicles.

> "We were told by HQ that jeep drivers were not permitted to drop our windshields due to the trip wires. They told us that a soldier had gotten his helmet taken right off by piano wire strung across a dirt road and it shaved his hair off just like he had gotten a crew cut. A little lower and he would have gotten his head cut clean off!"

From The Command Car

This part of the advance was slow moving and took several days. Between the snipers, artillery, mortar fire, planes and the mines, C-Company as well as the others attached to them, suffered heavy casualties. Pushing the Germans out of the forest was no easy task. It wasn't too easy for the Germans as well with some of their younger and more inexperienced fighter pilots misjudging the height of the trees in the forest. Mr. Libby recalls seeing a plane flying right into the top of a large tree as he describes what he witnessed.

> "It burst into flames and the pilot never made it out of his fighter plane. Dyda ran over to try and find the dead German pilot's pistol. I couldn't believe that Dyda was going over there to try and find his pistol for a souvenir. I thought to myself, he's going to get killed for a pistol? He found it, ran away from the plane and as he was looking at it, the plane blew up and burst into flames. He barely made it out of there alive, that crazy bastard!"

Peterson would fire the 50 caliber at the German planes as they flew close to the command car and Mr. Libby remembers how loud it was as well as the force of the gun on his vehicle. Always having to hold his hands over his ears when Peterson fired this big gun; Mr. Libby comments about those intense moments when they were in the heavier fire fights.

> "Bullets would be flying over our heads and I stayed down inside the car behind the plate iron. He would face the gun most of the time to the rear of the command car and shoot but the gun would be able to move a full 360 degrees if he needed. It was really loud! I couldn't tell if he was the one that

> shot down the planes or if it was a combination of everyone shooting at them when it would happen but he did his fair share of shooting. There were bullets and rounds flying all over the place. This was really a rough battle! It was one of the toughest times that I can remember. We fought all day and sometimes most of the night in that area."

The men of the 628th didn't have much time at all to relax during their time spent in the areas of the Hurtgen Forest or anywhere else for that matter. Mr. Libby recalls that when the B-Company needed a break, they moved in and when A-Company needed a rest, they moved in as well. They kept the rotation going and C-Company never got a long break to recover, they just kept moving and taking care of business day after day.

This proved to be one of the toughest battles they faced during the entire war. A brief break in the shooting at night would be a strategic move on the part of both sides to keep locations of troops hidden and prevent attacks in the darkness, but the unit was at the ready the entire time between the shelling exchanges.

> "I remember parking my vehicle under an apple tree one night as I stood on guard duty. A German plane would always fly over to try and draw enemy fire from us. We were told to *never* fire at him! We called him *Bed-check Charlie*. He was so close that I could read the numbers on the wing of his plane. He moved very slowly and I couldn't believe that his engine didn't stall out. He would fire some rounds down in several

> directions trying to get us to fire at him so that they could accurately lay artillery fire on us. I sat on guard behind the 50 caliber gun just wishing that I could shoot at him down. I could have easily gotten him but was told never to fire at him because it would give away our position. It was so frustrating to me and I always said, there is not enough time to get scared and if you did get scared, you'd flip your lid!"

One day while traveling out of the Hurtgen Forest, about a half a mile off of the road, the men of the 628th surprised an entire company of tired and weary German soldiers. The infantry surrounded them and took them as captive prisoners. They assembled the men and marched them to the road where they met Colonel Cole. He instructed the men to line the Germans up into one line and begin counting from each end to determine just how many they had just captured.

A soldier from the 47th who was walking the line as a guard noticed that a German POW within the line was making fun of an American GI. As the soldier made his second pass down the line, he struck the mocking German soldier with the butt end of his rifle right across his face. It knocked several of his teeth out of his mouth and caused it to bleed severely.

> "The German didn't know that the GI could understand German. He was making fun of the way he walked as he was on sentry. After he hit him, he looked at the German and told him that he didn't walk like the goose step; he walked like a human being. They took him out of the line and took him away to another

post in a vehicle that was going by at the time. None of the other German POW's made a move and no others decided to joke about the movements of the American soldiers after seeing that happen."

A sort of inventory of German prisoners was ordered by Colonel Cole. This attempt to keep some form of a count on how any they would be bringing to the area where they were being kept was normal but at times more time than they wanted to spend with these prisoners.

"The first count, they had 99 soldiers and then they did it again and got 100. I don't know where the extra one came from. They were going to do it again and Colonel Cole said to just take them back to the rear and forget about it. The top officer of the German unit started speaking to the men in English. We were all surprised that he spoke the English language so well. He told us that the German Luftwaffe was going to give us a good workout very soon. They kept this German Major separate and took him away with two of our high officers for interrogation and sent the others to the rear when all of a sudden, it hit us!"

It wasn't fifteen minutes later, the German planes started arriving overhead of the 628th. Two BF 109 Messerschmitt planes came in from the West, three came from the East and three came from the Southern direction with heavy strafing and dropping several personnel bombs down on the Americans, German soldiers and civilians alike.

"I heard the roar of the plane and hunted for cover! We all scattered to find a place to be safe. I was along the road and dove off into some pine needles and treetop limbs that were lying there. Two German prisoners dove in the same spot as well and landed right on top of me like a bunch of football players in a tackle. I told them; stay right there, they will have to hit you first! After the planes were done with their attacks, we all got up and started grouping the Germans back together.

Funny, none of them tried to escape, so we knew that they were all ready to quit! The two German soldiers that were on top of me got up, stepped into the road and returned to their line without any attempt of getting away. We were glad that the officer spoke up and told us what was going to happen so we could get just a little prepared for them."

The gunners of the 628th managed to knock down five of the German planes that created all of this havoc for the men and the remaining planes retreated back to German-held territory. With the tip from the German major, the men performed their jobs flawlessly and proved to be successful in this instance. Without the tip, it would had certainly been disastrous for the troops of Americans at this turning point of the war and certainly in this particularly heated battle.

Danger seemed to be everywhere and came in many forms, not only from the enemy, but at times, from within your own unit. A story that came to the mind of Mr. Libby during these interviews; describes a fresh GI just joining up with the C-Company.

Before the proper team of men whose specialty was to defuse bombs could arrive to any live rounds the boys would find, they would tape the area off indicating that this was not only a live round, but also that you were to stay back with any vehicles. The men had done such a thing to a German round which measured approximately two feet long that they had come across lying in a field. This fresh recruit walked over to live the round and picked it up. The other men watched in horror as he not only placed his own life in danger, but the lives of many soldiers around him.

```
"We had it taped off like a crime scene!
After the guy picked up the German 75 round,
he threw it off to the side into the woods.
He was a new guy who didn't know his ass
from a hole in the ground. This is why we
didn't get close to the new guys that would
come into battle. You had to baby them and
show them everything that they needed to
know. You should have seen us all scatter!
A platoon sergeant asked him if he wanted
to get blown to hell. He asked the sergeant,
why? The sergeant shook his head and just
walked away."
```

Another fresh soldier sat in the command car along with Libby and Peterson and watched an airburst which had occurred just overhead. These airbursts of course were beautiful in color due to the heat which was produced by the falling shrapnel. White, blue and red colors much like fireworks displayed on the fourth of July rained down as Libby and Peterson hid under the plate metal of the command car for as much protection as it could possibly offer to them.

> "I asked him, do you want to go home and see your mom and dad? He said yeah, why? I said to him, do you see that in the air? He said to me, yeah, isn't that pretty? I said back to him that its shrapnel flying all over. The next time you see that burst in the air, get under something! He was a nice kid but he sure was a stooge!"

The stooges were nicknames given to the new recruits that would freshly join the units. This was a tremendous responsibility given to any of the more experienced soldiers who were already in motion and had learned many of the ins and outs of the war. But still remembering how it was when they came into the theater as new recruits who were still wet behind the ears, the men took the time to teach the new stooges in case they were the ones that would help to save their lives one day. Loyalty to their unit and all of its members making them that much stronger was also a sign of their dedication to winning this war!

> "They pushed some of these new guys too fast. Six months and they were there in Europe to fight. It was just too soon for them and many of them got killed quickly because of it."

Another example of the newer soldiers being sent into the thick of the fighting too soon came when the men saw a military-type vehicle in this area coming down a road that had not yet been cleared of Germans and was still considered to be hot! As the sound of a large vehicle became obvious and coming straight toward the men of C-Company, the American driver came close to having an entire unit of men open fire on him.

> "This private was coming down a road that we had not cleared of the Germans that we knew

```
were out there somewhere. We heard this
half-track coming down the road and thought
we had some Germans coming down toward us.
We all got behind the 50 caliber and other
guns we had in the area and waited. As it
got closer, we yelled to the driver to halt
and then realized that it was an American
driver in an American vehicle. He stopped
quickly and looked really scared. We said to
him, man you almost got your ass shot off!
Don't you know that you were on a road that
is still considered hot?"
```

The scared and equally embarrassed driver told the men of C-Company that he was lost and was trying to find a unit that needed fuel. He was carrying several hundred gallons of gasoline on the vehicle and was basically a moving torch for the Germans that would had intercepted him on that road if he hadn't turned around where he did. He pointed to the road and said, *I don't belong there* and then pointed to another road and said, *I need to go there*. The guys of C-Company all got a big kick out of this guy and helped to point him in the proper direction, but not before commandeering several gallons of much needed fuel for their own vehicles. Mr. Libby finished this story with a little laugh by saying . . .

```
"I'm sure that he was very happy to give us
some gas in exchange for not shooting him."
```

Leaving the area of the Hurtgen Forest led the men into a valley which was populated with small homes in a little village setting. Shortly after staging the unit near some farmhouses, Charles needed to go to the rear echelon to get more 10-in-1 rations for his command car. During this short walk toward the supply truck, Charles heard the roar of a German plane nearing this small village. As the German fighter plane geared up to make it over the top of a tree, Charles noticed the plane zeroing in on a fuel truck which was near him. Charles kept walking to where he was going at a faster pace and heard the noises that would prove to be one of the closest calls to being shot and killed that he would receive throughout the entire war!

> "The good Lord Jesus Christ was watching over me that day. I never got excited, it happened so quickly! I didn't even run, I just kept on walking. The plane started strafing the ground to try and hit the fuel truck in front of me that was loaded with five gallon cans of gasoline. Bullets were hitting the ground on both sides of me. If he had banked to the left or to the right, I'd of been hit for sure! He only made one run by me and pulled up over some trees and then he disappeared. There must have been at least twenty rounds fired at me on both sides of my body. When I looked back, I could see the fire coming out of his wings. He knew he only had one chance to get it and that we had all kinds of guns sitting there that would get him on his next pass."

As Charles returned to his command car, back at the front of the staging area, several of the soldiers in his company who saw the incident continued to ask him if he was alright and if he was hit. Many commented that they thought he had gotten hit by the bullets and couldn't believe that he was still alive. They joked about the near-fatal experience but were glad that one of their own was safe and had made it through that close call unscathed. The men continued to joke with him while he as he walked back to his command car with the much needed 10-in-1 rations in hand.

> "It was a close call! I was glad that he was trying to hit the fuel truck and not me! This kind of thing was starting to happen so often that I didn't realize how dangerous this could have been. You get used to the shots and all of the noises when you've been around it for a while."

Aachen, Germany in the words of Mr. Libby was a hot spot full of excitement and heavy resistance from the German military. Small arms fire started the variety of noises that Charles heard as they approached the main area of battle. With increased artillery fire and mortar fire, it gave the 628th new challenges due to weather conditions as well as the terrain that led into this German occupied city. This city was also incorporated into what was known as the upper section of the *Siegfried Line*.

As C-Company became fired on and the battle became hotter, Captain Jones told Charles and Peterson to head back down the road past the rear echelon for a distance of approximately eight to ten miles to be clear of the main battle that was taking place. As the soldiers of the 628th fought to gain ground in this area, the command car driven by Libby headed to a much safer area on the command of the concerned captain.

> "I drove pretty fast until I got out of the distance that the rounds weren't as loud. Captain Jones didn't have to tell me twice to get the hell out of there! He told us to come back tomorrow morning. I drove until I found a shack that I had seen on the way into the city. It looked like an outhouse right off of the side of the road. I parked the command car behind the shack so that it was hidden from any passing Germans. We

got out of the vehicle with our carbines in hand and I went to the door and carefully opened it up. I saw two German soldiers lying on the floor that I thought were asleep. We waited a few seconds looking at them and didn't hear any breathing so I walked in and kicked one of them and he didn't move at all. We knew then that they were both dead. We each grabbed a soldier and drug them out of the shack and propped them up against the walls as if they were keeping watch for us. We went back inside and laid out our bed rolls and got a good night's sleep. The next morning when we woke up, we walked outside and said to the dead Germans, *good morning Fritz, good morning Hyrum* and loaded ourselves back into the command car and headed back to where we had left the others in our unit and to find Captain Jones."

As Charles and his radio man arrived back to the main battle area, they aided in the recovery for dead American soldiers. Captain Jones was happy to see both of the boys return in one piece. Charles told the story of their night of activity and the captain smiled at Charles after hearing the comical side of the story with their two dead German guards and the 628th moved onward in normal 628th fashion.

After staging in a new area down this long road, the unit was once again getting shelled by the German army. The Americans began to return fire at the Germans as it became a more heated confrontation. Colonel Cole was arranging the vehicles and the movement of the troops to keep them safer from the incoming barrage. A half-track was sitting in a breezeway of sorts and Colonel Cole told the two radio men in the vehicle to stay in the vehicle no matter what.

> "The fighting got hotter and the rounds started to hit really close to the half-track. The two GI's became scared and both got out of the vehicle and took cover in the barn that I was in. A few minutes later, a German shell hit the half-track and blew its contents apart including the radio and its entire payload, except the soldiers that were ordered to stay in their vehicle."

Colonel Cole was looking in that direction that the shell hit and saw the half-track burst into flames. With his head hung low, he said to the men that he had just lost two good radio men in the now burning half-track. Snickering from behind Colonel Cole ensued and he responded by looking angrily at the men and asking what was so damn funny about what just happened.

> "The two soldiers looked at him and said that *they* were the two guys that were supposed to be in the half-track. Colonel Cole smiled and said that he was damn glad that they disobeyed that order to stay in the vehicle and that he was happy that they were both alive."

Shelling continued throughout the night and the men had to find shelter which was safe as well as trying to find some form of personal comfort if at all possible. Charles and Peterson found an old winery nearby to take refuge. Located within this winery was an old coal bin that suited Charles just fine for his nightly slumber. Before taking that much deserved rest, the boys began searching around the building, as they always enjoyed doing, and found several bottles of wine. These two weary soldiers hauled some of the wine outside to have a little drink before they went to bed.

"We found out later that the wine was bad! We had drank quite a bit of many flavors like grape, cherry and others and we got sicker than heck shortly after that. We both hung our heads outside throughout the night and threw up violently. We could hear the shells hitting around the winery but didn't care too much because we felt so badly. We were both drunk and sick at the same time. A shell would hit in the mud and you could hear it being sucked down into the ground from the excess moisture. Another would hit a rock and would blow up.

I hated to think about the farmers that came along later that had to plow through the field where the ones didn't go off in that thick mud. It had rained there for several days and just made the conditions worse for all of our vehicles and especially our big tanks."

Americans were taken prisoner by the German armies just as we took prisoners of our own. The 628th were posted on a road just as they had done many times awaiting their turn to move forward into the next phase of the newest skirmish or battle that would most certainly begin soon when the order for a slow advance was given to begin moving into an area where they were needed. Colonel Cole received an improtant message from HQ. As he was riding in his jeep checking vehicle lines and the message came directly from the commander, General Hodges himself and demanded immediate attention from all of the men of C-Company.

"Colonel Cole got the call from *The Mustang* himself, General Hodges from HQ and asked him exactly where he was located. When Colonel Cole told him where we were, he told him that we were on the exact road that had been reported to HQ where there were four truck-loads of American POW's being taken somewhere by a squad of German soldiers. He told each of us in the convoy to get off of the road and to camouflage our vehicles right away and stand at the ready."

The unit all pulled off the road and began the chore of cutting tree branches to conceal their vehicles with a machete. Each of the drivers understood that they should be careful to hide the freshly cut sections of branches so that it did not tip off any German patrol that may be advance scouts for these trucks carrying the valuable payload of American soldiers. Upon total concealment of the vehicles, the men were instructed to get out and prepare to take the German vehicles on the command of Colonel Cole.

"We all got out of the vehicles, me included, except the radio man who stayed in the vehicles to get the order from Colonel Cole to make our move. He told us to wait until all four of the trucks were completely in front of us and then he would give the command. We heard the trucks coming toward us after about a half an hour. About fifteen minutes later, all four trucks were finally out in front of us and Colonel Cole came over the radio and said *"Take those bastards, they got our boys!"* Then, we all jumped into action and surrounded them."

There was nowhere for the Germans to pull off of the road or to turn around at that point. They knew that they had them completely boxed in with nothing to do except to fight or to surrender. Surrendering must had seemed the better option for these Germans as the men of the 628th came out of the woods from both sides of the road. The Germans knew that they were outnumbered and had no chance of winning this particular battle. And so, without firing a single shot, the Americans were free!

> "When they came down the road, there were three Germans to a truck. One sat on the hood of the truck and the other two were the driver and the passenger. We had them completely outnumbered and they wouldn't have had a chance at all to win if they hadn't surrendered to us. We were all very happy that it went off so well without anyone getting hurt or worse yet, killed."

Several of the men rounded up the surrendering German soldiers who threw their hands up and dropped their weapons. American soldiers moved them into one area with guards on them to prevent any attempt of escaping. At this point, the next phase of this operation would be to properly secure the American soldiers and check to see what type of physical condition they were all in.

> "These boys were suffering from severe malnutrition. They were all standing up and crammed in the truck just like sardines. They didn't have any room to sit down and were all very weak. Best I can tell is that there were 25-30 in each truck. They had been prisoners for quite a while and we

could tell that just by looking at them. They looked like skeletons with skin and their hair was very short and looked like it had been falling out. They were all in gray colored prisoner type uniforms with black stripes on them. Hell, they didn't even know that we were Americans yet! They didn't say anything at all to us. I think that they thought that we were Germans at first. One of the 47th looked up at some of the prisoners in the truck and asked them; *Hey, don't you recognize a GI when you see one?* Then he said to them, *We're American soldiers!* Over half of the soldiers started to cry immediately and started saying, *we're free, we're free* and *we're saved, thank God!* Then one of the American prisoners saw that a 47th GI had pulled out a flask of whiskey to take a nip in celebration and asked him if he could please have a swig. The soldier handed it up to him and he took a big drink of the booze. The second that he took the swig, he passed right out from having malnutrition. Another soldier caught the flask and none of the others took a drink of the whiskey after seeing what had happened to the first one. They did perk up a little bit and started talking to us about how happy they were that we saved them. Truth is, we were just as happy to have done it. It was a shame that there wasn't any news crew or film crew to help document this great event. I wanted people to know about it and hear

> what we did that day to save all of our boys that were suffering and probably would have died very soon from malnutrition or been tortured and shot in the German POW camps."

Drivers took control of the German transport trucks and turned them around to take the prisoners back to the rear echelon for questioning and ultimately back to England so that these brave Americans would receive the necessary medical attention that they truly needed.

> "Colonel Cole told us, you guys have seen enough, now get back to your vehicles and get ready to pull out! Back to business I guess, once again, no rest for C-Company."

Mr. Libby tells this particular story with many heart-filled emotions. Pride is the one word that pops into my mind as I hear his words and see his face while reliving this episode of the heroics which C-Company performed that day on a desolate dirt road in Germany.

> "This is one of my favorite stories that will be in this book and it's all the truth! There were close to thirty men in each truck and we saved them all. Our boys were safe and they were going home alive. It made me feel great to know that I was part of this operation. History didn't tell this story and I always thought it was a shame that these boys and C-Company weren't recognized for this."

As the command car driver, Charles was in charge of making sure that his vehicle ran without any types of mechanical problems. Along the path toward

Bergstein, Germany, Charles noticed that the engine was starting to miss and wasn't firing on all cylinders. Captain Jones instructed Charles to take the vehicle back to ordinance to have a new engine placed in this valuable transport vehicle. He told Charles that he would probably be there for at least three days and to wait there with the command car until the job was completed.

The first night in ordinance, Charles bedded down near his vehicle where it was staged for the mechanics of the unit to change the engine out on the very next morning. As Charles was resting and getting himself prepared for the night's sleep, he heard a noise coming from the hedgerow near him and stayed motionless. An officer from the unit tugged at his foot in an attempt to tell him that there were Germans in the camp.

```
"I actually heard both of them laughing, the
Germans. One was standing on the roots of
the hedges and the other was below him hold-
ing him up. The officer whispered, there's
Krauts in here. My carbine was still in the
truck. I hadn't gotten it out yet. I usually
keep right beside me every night in case I
get ambushed during my sleep. I couldn't
believe that they were laughing and being
so loud. The American officer shot his .45
through the hedges at the two soldiers.
They disappeared and fired a burp gun right
back at us through the thick hedges. This
was one of the few times that I got really
scared. I hid under the front wheel of the
command car for cover. I could hear the
bullets zipping through the grass past me
from the German burp gun. I wished that I
would have had my gun close to me at the
time. I really wasn't sure how many of them
```

> there were. The other officer that fired the pistol just rolled over and went to sleep like it wasn't anything big. Before I had crawled back into my fart-sack, I made sure that I had my gun beside me and that it was ready to fire this time! No other problems the rest of the night, thank God."

On the second night, some of the men were invited to sleep in a large house that was near the ordinance staging area. This was a much more comfortable sleeping arrangement for Charles without the chance of Germans trying to climb over the hedges to ambush him in his slumber. The very next morning, Charles was looking at the home and admiring the large fireplace that was located in the living room. He wondered if he would be able to see the sky if he looked up the large opening through its beautiful stone chimney.

> "When I looked up there to try and see the sky, I saw four ham quarters and two huge slabs of bacon hanging in there. Man did I hit the jackpot! They used the fireplace to smoke their meat and figured that nobody would find it way up there. I kept it to myself and on the third day there, the maintenance sergeant came to me and said, soldier, your vehicle is ready and you can go back to your unit now. I thanked and saluted him and he left the house. He was very polite to me. When the coast was clear, I crawled up the chimney where they had installed sheet metal to grab and climb up to hang their meats. I lowered a ham quarter and one slab of bacon to the ground and crawled back down out of the chimney. I hid

the meat in my bed roll and made my way to my repaired command car. When I got back to where my unit was, it was time to move out. Peterson and Captain Jones loaded into the vehicle and we were on our way to our next battle. I unrolled my sleeping blankets and showed them the find. I told Peterson not to say anything to anyone and I knew that Captain Jones wouldn't say anything anyway. I sliced a hunk of ham off for the both of them to enjoy and for the next few days when we were alone, we all had a special treat to eat."

The Battle of the Bulge is probably the most well-known battle of WWII and is captured in the memories of those who study this world event and especially to those who fought in it. For a command car driver, this battle produces memories of confusion, stress and not a minutes rest for many days on end of driving your officer from point A to point B continually in the heat of an ongoing and constant battle.

"The Germans pushed us back and then we pushed them back again into their territory. The Battle of the Bulge gave everyone on both sides a workout! It was cold and a lot of soldiers died there, on both sides. We fought day and night to get out of there. We had several days of artillery and tanks rolling around and exchanging fire. We also heard about the Germans shooting a large group of American soldiers execution style during this battle. We all felt bad that it happened to our guys and it made us all

> really mad. They would do anything, even murder. We took them prisoner when we could and they just murdered us!"

This battle was known as one of the worst in the entire war in Europe in respect to loses of equipment, weaponry and human lives. Weather played a major part in the troubles that each side faced. Troops met everywhere to fight for bits and pieces of land control. A concentration of Germans and Americans that converged in several cities that were connected, caused a *bulging* effect and there was nowhere to get away. This is actually where they got the name of the now famous battle.

Mr. Libby remembers that this time was very serious and the fighting was especially hot throughout this entire time the 628th was located there. He also remembers regrouping many times and also bringing in additional troops from France and other places in military trucks to aid in this deadly battle.

> "They unloaded them from the personnel trucks and sent them straight into the heart of the battle. At this point, it's sad to say, no prisoners were taken. We shot them all when we saw them and kept on hunting them down! There wasn't any time to do anything else and they were fighting as hard as we were. Tanks were getting blown up all around us, men were getting killed and I never knew which way to go with my vehicle. It was hell!"

After the conclusion of duty for the 628th at the Battle of the Bulge, movement at a pace that the 628th was now used to, continued to place them closer and closer to their next goal of being deeper into Germany. Just outside of the city of Cologne, the men of C-Company came across a large and ornate Catholic

Monastery. This building had been established as a medical facility for the Americans who were injured in battle. Several of the men also used this brief stop to take care of any of their medical needs they had sustained, resupply their company medical provisions and to make sure that no Germans were present in this important area for the Allies.

While in this monastery, Charles noticed that there was a German Major in the same room as the Americans. This was puzzling to him that a German officer would be there with our American troops. As the major turned toward Charles, he noticed exactly what had brought him there to this strange makeshift hospital.

> "He turned toward me and his face looked just like raw hamburger! It was a horrible sight to see. A French Guerilla fighter tapped me on the shoulder after seeing me look at the injured officer. I turned and looked at him and he motioned to the German officer and said in broken English, *I did that!* He seemed very proud and had a huge smile on his face when he told me. They waited for quite a while to get medical attention due to the fact that the Americans *always* got treated first. They must have really wanted to interrogate him to bring him in there with all of us. There was no way that he could even talk until someone put his mouth back together again, but I guess those are *the wages of war!*"

Latum, Germany provided a new temporary camp for the 628th. For about a three day period, the men stayed there until it was their time to move forward again. The first night there, Germans lobbed artillery shells close to their encampment but didn't hit anything important to the Americans who were temporarily staying there. On that second night, the German artillery continued near their camp, but it was getting closer. This alerted the officers and men alike to what could possibly be a spy within this town who was now giving much better coordinates to the Germans who were in the nearby city of Latum. According to Mr. Libby, drastic measures needed to be taken immediately to keep all of them safe! After careful consideration by the officers of the possible outcomes, a wise decision was made to protect the men and equipment of the 628th.

US tanks lined up and ready in Latum, Germany.

```
"We knew that there was a spy in the town
for the Germans. We kicked everyone out of
every single home in the town. We didn't
care who they were, we told them to leave or
we would blow their house up! Someone told
```

the Germans that we were eating there and staying for the time being. We had to do something to try and stop the shelling and we did it. Seemed a little extreme, but as I said before, this was war!"

After the German citizens were all out of their homes, the American GI's started a house-to-house search to find anything that would link any resident to the German army. Charles conducted his own search in his own methods which were usually to not only find out important information for the unit, but also to locate any item that would be useful or a comfort to his captain that traveled with him on the command car.

"I went into this really nice house and started to look around. I made my way upstairs and saw two large armoire's against the wall. After looking around the room, I thought to myself that there may be something behind them. I braced myself against the wall and pushed the unit away and immediately noticed that the wallpaper looked kind of funny. I was right! They had wall-papered right over a hidden doorway. I pushed on the wallpaper and it broke right through."

Charles found that behind the first one was what he referred to as a room that resembled a small, private hardware store. The small room contained everything from rakes to shovels to pick axes, wrenches, hammers, drills and many other items. In the far end of the room there were large Persian rugs hanging up which were a beautiful item that the homeowner was certainly trying to hide from the German army on their well-known scavenger hunts that they would conduct across the landscape to take back to Berlin for the Furor.

As he moved to the second unit, he found that it was covering a similar hidden room. All the while, Charles was armed with his carbine rifle in the event that there were German soldiers hiding within the home in just this sort of hidden room. As he started searching the contents, he noticed several medium-sized boxes stacked up against the wall.

> "I saw those boxes and wondered what was in them. When I opened the first one it was full of cigars! I couldn't believe that I had found all of these cigars. The first box I opened were too old and fell to pieces in my hand. I started to open the others and found some that were still good. I put one into my mouth to chew on and walked over to the window where I saw American GI's down below moving through the streets. I yelled out to them, *hey, any of you guys want a cigar?* They looked up and yelled back to me to throw some down. I threw some down to them, a box at a time and they were all very happy. They scrambled like ants to get to those cigars. I saw them putting them into their pockets one at a time and passing them out to all of their GI buddies."

Charles, in trying to protect the rest of the family's belongings, moved the armoire back to their original resting places and moved out of the house not revealing the contents to any other soldier. He made his way back to his vehicle with a box on his shoulder and loaded it into the command car. A soldier walking down the street was smoking a cigar as Charles passed by and he addressed him with a big grin on his face.

"I said to the GI, *where did you get that cigar?* He told me that some GI was throwing them out of a window back there. I looked at him, smiled and said, *that was me.* I showed him that I had some to and he thanked me for the cigars. He told me that there were guys twenty nine miles down the road smoking cigars now! I laughed and kept on driving down the road with a big smile on my face."

The great Jack Benny performing for the US troops just before the occupation period of WWII.

Kastl, Germany provided both the excitement of war and the excitement of a break from the action by means of a show for the GI's. The *Jack Benny Tour* came to Europe to entertain the American troops stationed there and in nearby camps. The city was still considered to be a hot spot for the Americans and caution was at its highest for everyone near this area. Mr. Libby remembers how exciting it was to learn of the show that was going to occur. He drove there from his location with a few buddies and upon arrival eagerly awaited the start of the show.

Along the path, he witnessed an old German man placing wreathes made of flowers on debris that lined the streets. Charles stopped his command car and called to the man in German asking him to come to his vehicle.

"I asked him in German, What happened and what was going on there? He told me in German and some broken English that the cities air raid sirens had not worked a few days prior to that and that when the Americans bombed, the citizens didn't have enough time to get into their bomb shelters and basements. The Americans thought that it was an industrial city and didn't know that the citizens were there without any form of alerting them to the bombing that would occur. He was placing these wreaths and flowers on the buildings and the rubble in honor of the more than one thousand German citizens that died there. I put my hand on his shoulder and softly said good bye to him in German and he nodded his head to me with tears running down his face. I guess that those are the wages of war and it happened sometimes. I felt really badly for him and all that died there. Then, I drove off to see the show with the buddies from my unit."

Appearing along with Jack Benny were two beautiful ladies of entertainment that enticed the GI's more than Mr. Benny. The famous movie star Ingrid Bergman was there as well as the talented lead singer for the Benny Goodman and Glen Miller Band, Martha Tilton. Mr. Libby fondly remembers that the show was very entertaining and that he also made a brave move that made it even more exciting than the others had experienced there earlier that day.

> "I went around the back of the stage and got close to the trailer that they had for the entertainers. I really wanted to meet Ingrid Bergman and get to talk to her. I found her there looking out the window which was wide open. I looked up at her and said, *good afternoon*. She looked at me and said; *Well, good afternoon soldier*. She asked me what my name was and I told her. Then she asked me where I was from and I told her Pennsylvania. Then we talked for a moment and she looked at me and said, *Well Charles, I hope that you get home safely*. I told her thank you and said that I hoped so too. I took a photograph of her for my scrapbook which I still have to this day. I told her that it was nice to meet her and she said the same to me and I went back to the show and watched the other performers. It was a neat thing to see them and to have a brief break from the war and all the fighting, but not for too long."

German shelling began to rain down on the area near the show and the performers were quickly evacuated by American troops. The GI's made their way back to their units and staged for any other incoming German attacks that were coming their way. Led by a command car out of the city, the van which held several of the performers and the private car which Jack Benny rode in made their way to much safer territory. This particular shelling at American troops would ultimately prove to be some of the *final* rounds that were sent toward the men of C-Company as the war was soon coming to an end.

Wessel, Germany was where C-Company crossed the Rhine River to make their final push to the Elbe River. A bridge where the unit would have been able to cross safely and quickly was blown out by the Germans and forced the men of this unit to call on the engineers once again for their area of expertise. It was time for the pontoons and the use of some good old American engineering to work for its military. During the assembly of these pontoons to build this temporary bridge for the crossing, some German planes made several passes to strafe the men and most of all, these valuable pontoons.

```
"When the Germans would hit one of the pon-
toons, the engineers would put another one
in right away! They were quick and really
knew what they were doing. We all sat and
watched them connect the pieces together and
it was really amazing how good these guys
did their jobs. We all appreciated those
guys for what they did."
```

One vehicle at a time, one tank at a time and after the entire unit had crossed, the pontoons were left there for any other unit to use when they arrived at that point. The men and equipment of C-Company were now across the Rhine River and when all assembled, the unit moved quickly to their next strategic location.

The war was nearing its end and in a time of little reporting of world events, to the men who were fighting this war, the most important announcement that ever came down the line would soon be passed onto Charles Libby. *"Hitler is dead!"* After the many assassination attempts on his life by his very own generals, after the many attempts by the United States military to bomb his many secret locations that he was believed to be hiding, in an act of true cowardice, he took his own miserable life! The official announcement on May 1st of 1945 was a welcomed one by many millions of people across the entire world, especially those who had put their lives on the line day in and day out during this massive collective effort to stop the man who seemed to be the Devil himself!

```
"When I heard that Hitler was finally dead
I thought that finally this war would come
to an end! I thought he was a coward af-
ter I found out he committed suicide. All
the guys were saying, that son-of-a-bitch
is finally dead! We were all glad that he
was gone and knew that soon after that his
generals would have to surrender to us. I
watched as many of the GI's celebrated and
cursed Hitler and what he had done."
```

For the 628th Tank Destroyer Battalion, at 0001 on May 9th of 1945, their fighting came to an end! C-Company was in Schmedenstadt, Germany at that time but for Charles Libby, it was still business as usual until he was physically on the ship to go home. Until then, he was a soldier and was still working and had a job to do taking care of the captain and making sure that his command car continued to make it in one piece from point A to point B.

Charles looked out for the officers he drove and the radio man, who also served an important job on his vehicle. It seems that if he could bring them any form of pleasure while fighting this war, he made sure to do it. Always looking for things that would make their lives just a little easier, Charles kept an open eye and fast hands to acquire these items whenever they presented themselves to him. This was war and the rules were slightly different than the ones that were observed back home in the states at that time.

The German army abandoned a wealth of equipment along the banks of the Elbe River when they retreated deeper into the motherland Germany. Half-tracks, weapons carriers, personnel carriers and miscellaneous items were all present along with the remains of several dead German soldiers that were part of the final battles at this area of the river. An American soldier from the 47th Armored Infantry had found a German radio which had a transmitter that enabled him to somehow pick up a frequency that played American music. Captain Jones heard the music coming from this particular radio and asked Libby if he and Peterson would go to the dike and try to find another of these radios. Without hesitation, Libby and Peterson loaded up in the command car and headed out on their scavenger hunt in hopes of finding what Captain Jones was hoping to soon acquire.

While searching the banks, without success, the boys found a large generator that could be used to hook up lights or other important necessities at their camp. While attempting to load this heavy generator with a rope, a nearby American GI was hit by sniper fire and Libby decided that it was getting too dangerous and too dark to be that far away from his unit. At this particular time of the war, the final peace treaty had not yet been signed and there were still several remaining elements of Germans that continued to fight hard and do whatever they could to disrupt the Americans, killing as many as they possibly could. Adolph Hitler was known to be dead and the thoughts of these American GI's were that the war was almost over and even though they were to still be on heightened alert, the war and all of its fighting would hopefully soon be over.

As Charles stepped up higher onto the dike, a German soldier suddenly appeared after walking out of a nearby barn. Libby reached to his hip with his left hand to pull out his pistol. Alarmed by the threatening motions of Charles, the German soldier threw his hands into the air yelling, "*Nik shootin, Nik shootin*", meaning *don't shoot, don't shoot*! Libby, speaking in German asked this surrendering soldier how many more were in the barn. The German soldier indicated in some broken English mixed with German that there were five more men in the barn and that they all wanted to surrender to the American forces and not to the Russians. Libby then asked if they had any more weapons other than the gun the soldier threw to the ground. The German then indicated that they had a few hand grenades, two rifles and one bazooka with only one remaining shell. Charles indicated to the soldiers to come out of the barn, surrender to him and bring out the remaining cache of weapons in their possession. Motioning for the soldiers to get their hands up, the German soldiers indicated that they understood his command and did so without any type of struggle or fight.

> "They seemed as if they were relieved for me to take them as prisoners. My radio man Peterson asked me if we were going to shoot them. I said to him, *Hell no! Hitler's dead and in week and a half the whole damn war will be over.* I told them that we'd take them back with us. They were very happy that an American had captured them knowing that they would be treated better than if the Russians would have taken them as prisoners."

In an act of human compassion for these German soldiers, Charles Libby cautiously loaded the six enemy combatants onto his vehicle to take them back to the temporary American encampment, but not without one more stern command to these now German prisoners of war.

> "I told them that I was going to take them back now and get up into the vehicle but if one of you makes a wrong move, as I pointed to Peterson, he's going to blow your head off with that 50 caliber. They indicated that they understood and that they weren't going to try anything. I was also very relieved

```
      that they were so cooperative and thought
      to myself, wow!, I just captured six German
      soldiers!"
```

The day was disappearing as Libby and Peterson were headed back to camp sadly without the requested radio for Captain Jones, but now loaded down with their important and very unexpected catch of the day. While driving along the darkened dirt road, a large collie dog ran out in front of the wheels of the command car. Charles had no time to swerve or to miss the dog and hit it head-on. The command car rose off the ground to one side and slammed back down to the ground killing the dog and terribly scaring Libby and Peterson. Thoughts of road mine, snipers and trip wires along these roads were always a though in the mind of Charles and the loud sound and tipping of the vehicle sent chills up his spine that he may had just hit one. As they came to a quick halt, Charles then asked Peterson if they had lost anyone. The startled radio man indicated that they had all joined arms and that they were all still aboard the vehicle and with a little over twenty miles remaining in the journey to get back to the camp, Charles was sure to pay closer attention to the roads as to keep the entire payload in tow.

As the vehicle made it back into town where the Americans were staged, they were greeted by Captain Jones shaking his head once again with a half grin on his face. He addressed Charles and asked him by asking; *Where the hell did you get those guys?* Charles told him the entire story and Captain Jones instructed him to drive them down the road to the American POW Camp that had been set up for these occasions.

```
      "I was laughing, Captain Jones was laugh-
      ing and many of the other soldiers got a
      big laugh over what I had brought back in-
      stead of the radio that he wanted. When I
      arrived at the POW Camp, I told them to get
      off of the vehicle and told them that they
```

> were at their hotel and there were all of
> their buddies. As each of the German pris-
> oners got off of my vehicle, they graciously
> shook hands with me and as the last German
> shook my hand, he looked right at me and
> told me in German that I was a good soldier.
> I paused for a moment and I felt very proud
> that I was able to turn these tired men into
> the camp and didn't have to kill them. They
> were brain-washed by Hitler and weren't all
> bad deep down inside."

A small tear runs down the cheek of Mr. Libby as he tells this story. The cracking of his voice also tells a story of a man that cared so much for others was able to give these men their lives without having to take it away from them. A mixed up time of war and of two sides being brought together because of a sick mad man and his own selfish goals and radical ideals.

POW's gathered, the dead being accounted for and the missing were still being searched for. Did all of the Germans know that Hitler was dead? Will all of the German soldiers and officers soon surrender? Is it all really over? All questions that raced throughout the minds of the American soldiers who had literally crossed the European continent fighting hard the entire way! Now what is in store for all of us? What is left for us to do here? Again, questions that would soon be answered by the high ranking officers and the superiors of HQ. Where will we go from here, home? How much longer are we all needed? Also, questions to be answered very soon and a new path for these men of C-Company and the entire 628th will begin. As for Charles A. Libby, more duty and time to be served . . . *From the Command Car.*

The Letter of Protection

* * *

FAITH, BELIEF IN A HIGHER presence and the power of prayer all have an impact on a person when placed in a stressful, dangerous or deadly situation. The contemplation of taking a life in the heat of battle, the indecision of your actions as well as finding pleasure in God's eyes are all in the everyday thoughts of a soldier. Prayer can give comfort to anyone in their time of need whether Christian, Jewish or a follower of any organized religious sect. A soldier keeps their faith close to their heart and builds another form of closeness and an open line of communication with their higher power during their time served in any conflict, police action or all-out war. Charles Libby was no exception to this common practice of faith during his time in WWII.

Having had roots in a small Pennsylvania town, the upbringing within a Christian household, attending Sunday school and his own personal belief in God, helped him to stay relaxed when it counted the most. Charles accepted what he was about to encounter and chose to be an example to those around him that may not have felt that they needed pray to and ask for help from that higher power, God himself.

Charles came equipped not only with his faith and his understanding of what prayer was, he also had one more weapon in his personal faith arsenal. He had brought with him a very dear and personal possession that he feels helped to protect him throughout every battle he faced. He had with him a *Letter of Protection* that was given to him by his mother Laura. This hand-written prayer, on a neatly folded piece of paper, was tucked away within the fold of his wallet and never left his side from the moment his mother entrusted him with it in the early 1940's and still to this very day. He carries it for a sense of spiritual protection and a clear reminder of his faith in God. It also reminds him of how the Holy Spirit stands beside us to protect us in times of our greatest personal needs.

Through our discussions, Charles told me that his Uncle Lyman Libby had also carried a copy of the very same letter with him into the many battles of WWI. The Libby family believed that this symbol and expression of faith, as well as living by these words, helped them to remain safe during each of their respective wars. He also believes that it helped the both of them to come home alive to their families without as much as a scratch. This letter of prayer was given to Lyman by his grandmother and it was believed from stories passed down that the letter was actually dropped from Heaven sometime in the 1700's and it's words were actually written in gold.

In further conversation with Mr. Libby in regards to this amazing letter of prayer and protection, he told me a story about his Uncle Lyman and a situation which he found himself in during a particular skirmish in France during WWI. When under extremely heavy artillery fire, Lyman Libby and his unit were forced to take cover in some thick trees. Lyman himself felt that he should run to the left to get into position and two other soldiers ran to the right side of the path. The two who ran to the right were directly hit and Lyman remained unscathed. This happened *many* times over throughout his service during his time spent in WWI. Lyman and the entire Libby family believed that he was protected by this special letter which he carried along with his strong conviction and unwavering faith in God.

With these powerful words of protection, Charles felt that he would *always* be protected because he truly believed when these words were spoken to God, they were not for any selfish reasons, but for good which needed to overcome evil. This powerful letter of protection and prayer reads as follows . . .

Letter of Protection

> "In the name of God, the Son and The Holy Ghost as Christ stopped at the Mount of Olives; all guns shall stop whoever carries this letter with him. He shall not be damaged through the enemy's guns or weapons. God will give him strength that he will not fear robbers and murderers nor guns or pistols, swords, muskets or bayonets shall not hurt him through the command of the Father, Son and the Holy Ghost. God be with him whoever carries this letter with him shall be protected against all danger and he who doesn't believe this letter may copy it, tie it around a dog's neck and shoot at him. He will see it's true whoever has this letter, shall never be taken prisoner or wounded by the enemy as true as it is that Jesus Christ died and ascended into Heaven and suffered on earth. He shall stand unhurt, injured by all guns and weapons on earth by the living God, Son and Holy Ghost. I pray in the name of Christ's blood that no ball shall hit him, be it gold or silver and that God in Heaven may deliver him from all sins in the name of the Father, Son and The Holy Ghost. It fell from Heaven in Palestine in 1728. It was written in gold letters, AMEN."

The words of this letter of protection still bring an overwhelming source of energy and power into Mr. Libby. He reads it with great pride and an even greater amount of faith in the words themselves. I myself could not pass up the opportunity to study these words and hand write a copy of this prayer to carry with me. Tucked away within the folds of my own wallet, the same letter as Mr. Libby had carried more than seventy years ago is carried by myself.

Another convincing argument to the power of this letter, faith and prayer, Mr. Libby spoke of a time when the men were getting ready to meet destiny head-on. While relaxing one day in Aachen, Germany in an old blown out gymnasium, the men of C-Company were killing time and waiting for orders to move out. Charles mentioned this powerful letter and gave each of the other soldiers the opportunity to copy the letter for themselves and draw from their own personal faith and the protection of this powerful letter of prayer. As the men were all collecting their personal possessions and packing them carefully within their US Army issued duffel bags; Charles took upon himself to tell the other GI's the amazing story of his Uncle Lyman and how he also carried it. He told them that he wasn't sure if it would work for them, but why not copy it and have God on their side. He explained to the men that he truly believed it and that he had strong faith in God. Four of the soldiers who were there at the time also agreed that it could be true and that they wanted to make copies of this powerful letter.

```
"One soldier named DiOrio decided that he
didn't want any part of it. He laughed at us
and asked us if we really believed in that
stuff. I told him yes and asked him what he
had to lose by copying it. He just laughed
at all of us and said, if you believe in
that stuff, you are all crazy and he walked
away."
```

During the very next battle in Aachen, DiOrio panicked and got out of his vehicle and started to run back toward the American line during the fire fight instead of fighting hard next to his fellow soldiers of C-Company. The reports from other American soldiers state that shortly after he lost his nerve and ran away from the enemy and he was shot four times in the back and killed in action. The four other soldiers who copied the letter that day *all* survived the long hard battle without as much as a scratch.

Faith, speculation or just a tall tale from the days of war or the power of God and his protection over those who call on his power with their faith? Whatever your assumption of the facts, it happened and leaves no room for debate as to what the results were for the men that copied and carried that letter with them into battle. This is a story that can be found nowhere else in the historical content of WWII that we know of, but this is a true story that happened in the world of Charles Libby and the men of C-Company while they were serving their country in the heart of a world war. Charles, from behind the wheel of his command car believed in it, carried it, passed it onto others and most of all, was protected to tell this story over seventy years later in his blessed and happy life at the age of 97 years!

"I'm not trying to brag or say anything against the good Lord. I just think that he would want for me to tell people about this *Letter of Protection* and to pass it on so that others will copy it, carry it and believe in it just like I did during my time in WWII. I never took it out to read it other than the times I passed it onto other soldiers. I knew I had it, I knew what it said and I knew that what it said was going to protect me through the words of the Almighty God! Amen!"

Occupation of Europe

* * *

THE OCCUPATION PERIOD IN THE Europe Theater by the allied forces was the next step to the stabilization of this part of the world. American and British soldiers alike felt a huge sigh of relief as their duties became that of a police force rather than a fighting force. German citizens who didn't fight against the allied forces became local military police to help protect their own citizens and remaining homes. US troops oversaw the local police forces and offered training to help them reorganize and restore some form of normalcy within their war-torn lives.

As American soldiers went home; the Germans slowly took over their duties. Although some GI's stayed for an extended amount of time, it was the belief of the allied forces that most of the German citizens were innocent of the many atrocities that Hitler's officers committed and shared none of his inhumane and radical beliefs. American soldiers also felt a strong sense of fear within the German citizens that they met during their time spent on their soil.

The German Reich had controlled the movements and the very thoughts of its entire population. Citizens would disappear prior to and during the actual time of the war if they attempted to speak out against the Furor or any of his personal beliefs or political policies. So, much like zombies and well-manufactured brain-washed slaves of thoughts and actions, the German citizens did what they were asked of them to stay alive and protect every single member of their precious families.

"You knew that the people were scared and had suffered because of what Hitler did. We didn't have to worry too much about the adult men and women that we met and interviewed but we really had to watch the younger ones very closely. *The Hitler youth* were brainwashed and if you would turn your back on them, they might had killed you. This is what they had been taught their entire lives and even their parents were scared of them at times. Hitler went as far to tell the citizens that the Americans would kill the men and rape their women. That simply wasn't true and it took some of them a while to get used to us being there and to actually trust us."

Occupation wasn't without its unknown dangers. Land mines and booby-traps were left behind by the German forces to do as much damage as they could inflict long after they were done fighting. Remaining German and Axis forces who either didn't know the war is over or still wanting to take revenge for the Furor by killing Americans, was not uncommon to find in their daily movements. With all the unknown dangers, the allies were most certainly still at high risk of attacks during this period of occupation and policing. Along with these dangers, many stories remained untold about the occupation period and some of these stories will add another element to the history books.

In this chapter, Mr. Libby shares memories of his time spent in Germany on occupation that are either new historical additions, humorous tales, noteworthy happenings, compassionate deeds or shocking stories that needed to be told. The first of these stories fits into the category of shocking and takes place at the shores of the Elbe River.

The Americans were instructed by General Eisenhower to stay put at the Elbe River and the men of C-Company were thankful for this break to say the least. History books have its accounts and stories of why they were there and for how long but this recount of a situation at the Elbe itself has been locked away in the mind of Mr. Libby and many other soldiers that lived it during those few days at the river banks. He may be the only living American soldier today that experienced this particular event. Not something that the press covered for the purpose of keeping peace between our two nations and the public's perception of how the allies worked together during the time spent fighting together or maybe a story that was hidden by the commanders on the ground for fear of being court-martialed, but it happened there none-the-less.

With the Americans on one side of the Elbe River and the Russian troops on the other side, strategically they had that area sealed up and totally fortified against any type of German resistance. But, seemingly not very secure against one another. As rumor has it, the Americans and the Russians may have fought together sharing the same goals of defeating Adolph Hitler, but their goals were different and their relationship was not all roses. Tension between the two forces and the notion that each was as good as the other escalated at the Elbe River and each tested their might by flexing their muscles.

```
"We had things that they knew we had and
they wanted them. Also, they had things
that we would had enjoyed having as well
while we all sat there doing nothing at that
river bank."
```

One evening, soldiers from the 47th Armored Infantry on the Western side of the Elbe River loaded themselves into a small row boat which the Germans had abandoned to cross a narrow part of the river. To see if the Russians would make a trade with them to acquire some of their well-known Russian vodka as well as make friends with some of them, the American soldiers made their way across the river making no attempt to be quiet or conceal themselves. Some of the

Russian soldiers opened fire on this small boatload of American GI's that night and it did not set well with the American forces there at all!

```
"They knew that we were there across from
them and that no Germans would be coming
across that part of the river right be-
tween us. Those cocky bastards just wanted
to show off and start some trouble with us
as usual."
```

The American soldiers made a hasty retreat back to the safety of their shoreline without firing a shot back toward their *supposed* allies. The tempers of these 47th Infantry men who have been hardened in battle ran hot. They sat on the shoreline the next day camouflaged waiting for the moment that the Russians would try to come across to their controlled side of the Elbe River.

About a week later, some Russians soldiers decided to come across in their own small boat. The 47th returned the gesture by firing at the Russian soldiers wounding one and killing another. Three days later, a high ranking Russian officer accompanied by four gun bearers carrying automatic machine guns made their way across the river to the American side to meet with the American officers to discuss the events that unfolded just a few days before.

The officer was in his full uniform with all of his decorations from the war adorning his chest and shoulders. The officer was taken to the colonel who was in charge at the time and stated his case; very upset about what had happened. Unknowing to the Russian officer, the young American colonel spoke perfect Russian. The American officer paced back and forth looking to the ground with his hands on his hips listening as the upset officer as the Russian officer spoke to him. Mr. Libby indicated that when the Russian officer had finished his passionate rant, thinking that he was intimidating this American officer, the colonel spoke back to him in his native language telling him something that he didn't want to hear.

"He said to the Russian, *Those are the wages of war. Sometimes you win some and sometimes you lose some.* His eyes got really big and none of us could understand what he was saying at the time but knew that it was upsetting him greatly. He continued to say that your guys shot at us and missed ours and our guys shot at yours and killed one. That is what happens in battles. He told us later that he followed up with telling him; *Now you can get back into your boat and paddle across yourselves or you can be lying dead in the boat and we'll paddle you back.* He ended it by telling them to get the hell back across where you belong and we won't bother you and you don't bother us!"

The Russians all turned away and quickly walked back to the shoreline and got back into their small boat and rowed themselves back to the Eastern side of the river. For the next two weeks, the units kept to themselves but watched a little closer as to the security of this section of the Elbe River. The American GI's were told by the officers not to agitate the Russians. This is a story that is both shocking and unbelievable at the same time about two forces that were there to prove their might and their dominance in the time of war. Some would say it was one of the first steps leading to the cold war and others would say it was merely a case of mistaken identity. Needless to say, it happened and tells another story of the horrors of war and that each day offered surprises from both friend and foe.

Witzenhausen provides a story which can go into the historical category while on occupation in this German city. Some of the men of C-Company were gathered around the command car when a German soldier in an officer's uniform walked into their camp. The German soldier immediately threw his hands up and spoke in broken English to the American GI's. Now with three guns pointed at him, he started to carefully explain that he had important military information and indicated that he was a friend and asked them not to shoot once again in the broken English and German mix.

The men, including Mr. Libby, allowed him to speak and saw that he was not a threat to their safety.

```
"I yelled at the soldiers near my vehicle
not to shoot! One guy had thrown a bullet
into the chamber to kill him. I told them,
the guy can speak good English, let's listen
to him."
```

He proceeded to tell the men of the secret plans that he was carrying with him that described the designs of jet propulsion rockets that he had developed for the German Air Force and was bringing these to the Americans to help them and that one of the high officers of the United States Army in their camp was waiting for him and would be there to pick him up to take him somewhere upon his arrival.

Several men all gathered around Charles's command car as the German soldier began to show some of the documents and plans to the GI's that he had with him. He also indicated that he would be going to the United States and that he would even beat this group of American GI's back to their own homeland.

```
"He started to show us some of the stuff he
had with him and then the Provist Marshall
pulled up with two MP's and started talking
to him. They said to him; Are you ready to
go sir? We couldn't believe that our officer
called him sir. He said that he was ready
and told us all goodbye, shook all of our
```

```
hands, climbed into their command car and
they all drove off. He was a really nice
guy and we could also tell that he was very
intelligent. We didn't realize until much
later just how important that German sol-
dier was to the US Army that strolled right
up to my command car!"
```

As the author of this book, I write stories in this manuscript and I am always amazed of what I am told by Mr. Libby. I enjoy all the stories of what he experienced while in WWII. This particular story really caught my attention so I started digging into the historical background of people who may have been in this area and who it may have been that he had his brief encounter with that particular day. After searching for photos and any information that I could possibly find, it came time to show Mr. Libby the photo which I found in an archival reference to V-2 rockets. As I showed him the photo, his face lit up and he said to me, *Where did you find that?* Then he told me to my surprise and hopeful anticipation, *That's the guy!* I became even more excited about the find that I had just come across. The photo of the man that I showed him was of one of the most important and intelligent men that ever lived and added one of the most exciting and beneficial contributions to our air force and modern aviation. The man in the photo was none other than Werner Von Braun! This man invented the V-1 and V-2 rockets and the technology that advanced manned flight which even led up to the development of NASA's Space Shuttle!

The first time that Mr. Libby spoke of this story, he told it to me in a nonchalant manner. I immediately sat up in my seat and proceeded with more in depth questions and scolded him for not telling me the story earlier in the interview process. We both got a laugh out of it and I made sure from that point on that the story would get into the book and add a new twist on the now known historical truth to who Von Braun actually surrendered to and that the men of C-Company had something to do with it but were never recognized.

"I was glad that I happened to be there. Many didn't even get a chance to see this guy in our company. He wasn't there too long and we really didn't know how important this guy was to the US military, especially the air force. When we saw the Provost Marshall and the MP's come for him, we sure were glad we didn't shoot him or we would have all been in big trouble!"

The rest is history and this story can now be added to that important part of the information puzzle! A lot of vital information during this time may have been distorted for certain reasons to give credit to people that may or may not have been there. Written history tells it differently than Mr. Libby, but this twist brings him and several men of the 628th C-Company into this important picture for those brief moments. The story that comes from Mr. Libby is his recall and I have no reason not to believe that it was true. He didn't even realize just who it was until I showed him the photo and explained exactly who this man was. So, in a nut-shell, I will make a very bold statement that I also believe to be true . . . *"Mr. Charles Libby, in stopping the soldier from shooting this German officer that day, literally SAVED our space program as we know it today!"* Take it as fact or believe others, but we offer this story from someone that was there and has kept it stashed within his memories for all of these years to now share as fact.

Heiligenstadt, a spa town in Germany, was one of the first places that these men actually got to take a big breath and well deserved rest. Always on the move, occupation was a welcomed change of pace for these weary American soldiers. Early in the occupation of Germany, US GI's began their new role in the European Theater of policing, rounding up the last of the German soldiers and officers for trial and punishment as well as cleaning up their remaining gear, damaged vehicles and any other equipment to ship back to the US military bases.

As groups, the GI's were appointed to certain houses to do random inspections in an effort to check for certain items that would now be a crime for them to be in possession of. A note was given to the residents in each town to describe these items and exactly what to do to be in compliance with the new laws of the occupation. Some of these items included pistols, rifles, transmitter radios and any type of military maps or German military equipment. If the citizen had any of the outlawed items, they were required to bring them to the US soldiers, if not, this note also told them that they would be severely punished if they did not comply. This particular note also told the German citizens that they would not be harmed in any way and that if any of their personal items were to come up missing, they were to report it to the officer of that particular group that inspected their home.

"There were six groups of us that were chosen to do work there from all of the companies, each one was led by a sergeant. We moved from home to home and proceeded to search the entire area which produced several of these items with no resistance from the German citizens about turning them over. One of the German women in that town came out of her home and alerted the sergeant that something was missing from her bedroom. She told them that her diamond earrings, bracelet and a choker were now missing after the American soldiers inspected her home. Right away, we all were to assemble with our groups for this particular shakedown because something had come up missing. The next morning we all stood with our groups lined up at attention, cooks and all. A captain started reading the Articles of War to us and nobody was permitted to

```
leave the building until he was finished
reading all of them. When he finished, he
thanked us all for listening and he told us
all to go back to our units."
```

The soldiers all knew that there was something terribly wrong after hearing this speech.

An immediate investigation was started to find the correct group that was in her home. After determining which of the groups was searching her home, officers went to their barracks and began their own search, uncovering the missing items in a soldier's bed roll. Upon finding these valuables, the soldier was taken away by MP's and charges were filed for violating the Articles of War. The woman got her jewelry back and the Americans continued their business at hand, which was to find items that were now considered to be illegal for these citizens to possess.

```
"We never saw that guy again and nothing
was stolen from another home after that!"
```

The searches produced more than just weapons and radios. Further searches within Heiligenstadt produced something much more horrible than what was used against the American soldiers. One such search was conducted within a German school house. This particular search found that this building was housing several young German women numbering about thirty and that they were being held there against their will by German officers. These young ladies were told to stay there and that they were never allowed to associate with any American soldier that they may encounter or that they would be killed. The German officers themselves were using all of these poor young girls for both sex and slave labor.

```
"When we got there, they were very happy
to see us. They didn't even know that the
```

```
Germans had left the area or that the war
was over! They told us in their broken
English that the German officers would hit
them and that they forced them to have sex
with them. It was sad and we were glad that
we were able to help free them from this
horrible ordeal. The Nazi's told these girls
that Americans would kill their men and
rape them. They cheered for us when they
knew that we were in charge now and that
the German officers would never be back
again to harm them."
```

This is just one example of the mindset of the Germans and how their unquenchable desire for anything they wanted ruled their citizens and served their own sick perversions. This occupation was a symbol to the German citizens that it was over and that they could now breathe again and finally start to reassemble their broken lives.

Unfortunately, not all of the German citizens shared the enthusiasm of having Americans still there on their soil during occupation, especially the youth that have been influenced by Hitler since their early school days. As previously mentioned, the brain-washing techniques that were used on them were effective and they remained a serious threat to the soldiers on the ground trying to reassemble their society and get them onto a path of normal life, reconstruction and future prosperity.

One day while on guard duty and walking sentry, Charles noticed two German teens on a bridge close to their location. One of these two youth were mocking Charles and his fellow GI's as they walked the area doing their required job of making sure that all was well in that zone. Taking notice to this disturbing behavior, Charles left his post and flanked the youth, sneaking up behind them. He startled them and asked them in German what they were doing and what was wrong. The youth turned to Charles facing him as the other GI's watched Charles do his thing.

> "I asked them in my broken German, *what's going on*? They looked at me and said that all was well. I told them to get off the bridge and get home and don't come back around! I stared them right in the eyes. They didn't talk back and they knew that I meant serious business."

The German citizens were to be protected by the American soldiers and any type of threat from within their communities and their citizens who may have been Nazi sympathizers were to be dealt with sternly. Charles let them go without any further action and these teens now knew to allow the Americans do their job and to not try to start any trouble with them.

Another occasion while on watch, Charles was accompanied by a sergeant in the town of Witzenhausen. As the German citizens filed by going about their normal business, Charles noticed something that looked out of place among the crowd. There were two nicely dressed young men who were approximately nineteen years of age walking through the street. They wore a clean white shirt which looked to be pressed and each had a pair of dark black dress type pants. As the young men approached the American soldiers, they became unusually nervous and increased their speed and pace as they walked. Charles immediately pointed out what he had seen to the sergeant who accompanied him on this particular watch.

> "I said to the sergeant, do you see them? He looked at the crowd and said see what? I pointed to the two young men and told

him that they had on shirts and pants like the Hitler youth that were in the German army and could still be a threat. We went to them and asked them to come with us and sat them down on a curb off to the side of the street. We started to ask them questions and then asked them to stand up and take their shirts off. When the young men raised their arms, they had the lightning bolt tattooed under their arm as a symbol of being a part of the *Youth Squad*. I was glad that I was paying close attention to this crowd of people and that I saw them or they could have slipped by the both of us."

The MP's were called to this position and the two were taken to a base for questioning. This job that the Americans had during the time of occupation could not discriminate ages of the people that they were to question or arrest. Hitler used anyone he could to perform his dirty work and it usually started with the youngest who would grow up with the mindset of a mad man; making it that much easier to control them even into their adult lives.

Any free time for the American soldiers who were on occupation was spent thinking about their homes and when they would ultimately get to load their ruck sacks and tired bodies onto the ship to take them there. Still hardened by war and ever wary of their surroundings, many of their activities still showed a display of their military training. One such activity was hunting for the local species of deer which lived in this particular forest which Charles was stationed during this point of the American occupation.

Charles would take his command car to the top of a hill near a watering hole during the evening hours. Having been an avid deer hunter back in the woods of Pennsylvania, he was no stranger to the habits and movement of these tasty animals.

Perched on the plate iron of the command car with either his buddy Peterson or Bik and sometimes both, they would all sit and watch for glowing eyes of a deer in the night. When they would see them, to be quite sure that it was a deer and not American soldiers, the lights of the command car would be turned on and the shot from a carbine rifle would soon follow, dropping the deer in its tracks.

Deer harvested by some of the 628th in Germany.

"The Burgermeister, the mayor of the village, went to our Provost Marshall, the head MP, with a complaint and asked him if we would stop shooting all of their deer. We'd get almost four a night because we were such good shots. They were much smaller than the ones I had shot in Pennsylvania. He was afraid that they weren't going to have any deer after we left the area. We ate everything that we shot and also gave a lot of the meat to the people in the villages, so it never went to waste. The Germans would follow us and if we didn't want the deer that we shot they would take it. I saw one German guy load a buck up onto his bicycle and ride down the road to take it home. We slowed down our hunting after that and had to find some other forms of entertainment to keep us busy because he told us that we could only shoot one deer a month."

The next story of the period of occupation fits into two categories by being both humorous and amazing. While taking sand bags out of the command car that lined it to help with the explosions of road mines, a GI from Charles's company decided to try something that he had heard about with his pistol. The scenario was that if you took your .45 caliber pistol and held it tightly to your hand and tried to pull the trigger, the pistol would not fire. He decided to try it, but with using a German pistol that he had acquired along his journeys rather than the .45 caliber.

"I was standing right beside him when he tried it. He placed the German pistol to his hand and pulled the trigger. It didn't make a loud bang like it should, but it *did* go off. He looked at me and said see Charlie I told you. I was shocked that he actually did it. He showed me his hand and we didn't see a thing. It happened so fast that he didn't even realize that it didn't work right for him. The bullet went right through his hand and when he put his arm down beside his body the blood started dripping down his fingers. He felt something wet and pulled his hand up and saw the fresh blood from his hand. He looked at me and said, *I guess I better go to the infirmary.* We were both laughing and I looked at it and asked him if he wanted me to go with him. He smiled and said, *no, I'll be ok.*"

The amazing part of this story was that when he pulled the trigger, the barrel of the gun was pointing right at the belly of Charles. The two men looked all around the ground to see where the bullet hit before he went to get aid and could not find the point of impact anywhere! Was this another amazing testimony to the *Letter of Protection* that Charles was carrying in his billfold from his loving mother? Was this another form of proof that the letter worked for him during the war? In the mind of Mr. Libby, it most certainly was! There was no other explainable reason why the bullet should not had hit him other than the protection that Charles received from this special gift. Make your own assumption, but in his mind, he feels that the good Lord had watched after him every step of the way, even from a careless American soldier.

"Years later at the reunion here in the states, I asked him how his hand was and did it turn out alright. He shook it around and moved all of his fingers and said it worked

> out really well. He pointed to the woman beside him and told me that he met his wife as a nurse at the hospital there in Germany. I smiled and said, well, I guess it did turn out alright for you after all."

The ending of American occupation for the soldiers who fought the major battles was a sweet moment for these brave men. The soldiers that had driver's licenses could take a vehicle and head toward France via the Autobahn. Drivers would shuttle the soldiers back to the camps closer to the base that they would ultimately ship out of to return to the states. Soldiers would see some of the desperation of the German people that they would leave behind as a lasting reminder to these Americans during these runs.

> "At this base in Frankfort, German citizens would hold an empty plate up to the fence that surrounded this particular camp. They knew they had to stay behind the metal cable that was strung up at the camp. The cooks started making extra-large portions because they knew that we were feeding some of them that *really* needed the food. If they saw a GI near the fence, they would try to approach them to see if they would share their food and most of the time the GI would give them some."

While transporting these men and vehicles toward La Havre, France, Mr. Libby vividly remembers the rows and rows of vehicles, planes and massive amounts of military equipment just waiting to be shipped back to the United States along with these GI's. It was getting closer and closer for many of them to finally be home and Charles was no exception to the excitement that filled the air with everyone's anticipated journey.

A story of compassion takes place while in Heiligenstadt, Germany after the pull-back. While driving to do another pick up, Charles noticed an old German man who was limping through the street. He noticed that his legs were in a very bad way and possibly eaten up with gangrene. Charles had seen so much death, sadness and destruction that if he could, was ready to help anyone that he was able to. He offered to load the old man's wooden cart onto his vehicle that he was pushing while in this great pain. This home-made wooden cart was old and only had two wheels remaining. This cart was loaded down with his remaining worldly possessions after the fighting had ended which had previously destroyed his home.

```
"I told some of the other soldiers standing
there that I needed help to load the cart
on my vehicle because the old man could
hardly walk. They all proudly chipped in
and they loaded it onto my car and the old
man leaned in the assistant driver's side
because it was hard for him to stand or sit
with his legs in that condition. Family met
him where I dropped him off and some other
soldiers helped to get the cart off of the
vehicle. The old man got tears in his eyes
and thanked me in German. I guess that this
was his new home and he was glad that we had
taken him there."
```

Another act of kindness from Charles to the people of Germany that had no part of Hitler's gruesome rampage. This touching story is still in the forefront of his mind as he fondly remembers the German citizens he interacted with during the war that most wanted no part of.

In an effort to keep the moral up with the American GI's and to show the German people that their lives could get back to some form of normalcy, the women of Witzenhausen were invited by the US Army to come and dance with them in the make-shift base in a large German building which was used for the Communications Center and the offices of Sgt. Luckey. They would be dancing with the eager GI's who were now stationed there.

> "We were excited when we heard about it. Of course, I loved to dance very much and this was a great opportunity to meet the local German women on a more personal level now that the fraternization rules had been fully lifted by HQ."

Up to this point in time, there was a strict rule for the soldiers of no fraternization outside of their normal duty with the German citizens. A young German boy used to watch Charles as he would maintain his command car and enjoyed watching him drive away on his regular chore to go into the main city of Witzenhausen to pick up mail for the company as well as other forms of communications for Sergeant Luckey and his full staff of officers.

When this rule had been lifted and things were more relaxed, Charles asked Sergeant Luckey if it was alright to take the young German boy with him to pick the mail up in his command car that he had admired so much. He allowed it and told Charles to keep the plate armor up and not to make it too noticeable to the others within the city. The young German boy enjoyed this activity very much as well as his time spent with Charles. It was special for the both of them after what they had both endured for so long.

When the dance was announced, the young boy repeatedly asked Charles to meet his mother and to dance with her when they attended this much anticipated social event.

> "When I got there, the young boy was at the building with his mother. He said hello

Charlie and continued to ask me to dance with his mother. I asked him to point her out and he did. She was dancing with Dyda at the time and after I saw her, I told him to go and tell her in German that after she was done dancing with him to come and see me. She was really pretty and I wanted to meet her and found out later that she had been watching me and wanted to meet me as well. After we were introuduced, we spoke and danced several times that night and we started seeing each other after that night of the dancing. I really enjoyed spending time with her while I was there in Germany. She asked me more than once to come back to Germany after I was out of the Army. I never went back, but I often think about her and her son fondly."

This time of war separated many people with an ocean between them. The war also brought people together in many ways, only to be separated later much like their families who were back in the US or the family member that died during the fighting. Bitter sweet emotions and stories from WWII have been told in many ways. This particular story leaves us with the feeling of what could have been if Charles would had returned for a woman that loved him and a young boy that was in need of a father like Charles. The thoughts still appear in the mind of Mr. Libby as he comments to me that she was very nice and *I wonder if* . . . and then he stops there with a long pause and a big smile on his face.

It seems that in an effort to forget about the *Dear John letter* that he would have to deal with upon his return, he found himself breaking a few hearts in Germany. Another female caught the eye of this American soldier named Velma Strousmand. This successful German woman owned three houses in Germany as well as a chocolate factory. Enthralled with Charles and without word from her husband who disappeared in the war years before, this attractive and successful woman wished for the young Charles to remain with her or to return right after being discharged from his military service with a heart-filled promise to take care of him however he required upon his return.

Sadly, Mr. Libby still wonders what would have become of this arrangement as well and a relationship with the beautiful and exotic woman from Witzenhausen, Germany and how his life may have gone upon his return.

```
"I thought about it a few times but decided
that my home was in the United States with
my family and I had to take care of myself
just like I had done all along in my life.
I still think about her often and wonder if
she is still alive today like me."
```

On the humorous side of the stories of war which came from the mind of Mr. Libby, was about a soldier named Joe Malvestuto. One day Charles came across this friend with German money hanging out of both of his pants pockets. This GI had found a large sum of money in one of the bombed out buildings that they had just checked for the possibility of any remaining German soldiers.

```
"He was afraid that he wouldn't be able to
get out of the country with all of these
German marks so he started giving it all
away to other GI's as a sort of joke. He
figured that it wasn't going to be worth
anything when he got home except for toilet
paper. Boy was he wrong!"
```

After giving much of this money away, a soldier explained to him that he would be able to turn in up to five-hundred dollars in La Havre, France to the exchange office and take that money home with him. Experiencing some embarrassment and shock, this soldier had given away a small fortune to the other soldiers as simple German souvenirs.

> "He didn't think ahead to work it out with all the other guys to give them a small cut if they would each go and get their five-hundred dollar limit for him. All he could say was that he had given away a small fortune! We all were laughing at him but he didn't think that it was too funny. At one time his pockets were filled with money and it was even hanging out of each one. He never gave me any money, but I saw what had happened to him."

Men were held to a standard while wearing the uniform of a United States soldier. Limits of money and limits to the possessions were all in place to protect the German citizens and to maintain the integrity of our fighting forces. They were there to defeat one tyrant and the United States military made sure that the German people couldn't label our troops as being one in the same.

Mr. Libby brought home a few items from the war that would be a reminder of what he had done. One of these items that reminds him of the terrible conquest of a man that wanted to consume everything he surveyed is a Nazi youth armband. Charles knew what these meant and saw many of them around the arms of the men who were shooting at his unit and many of them on the arms of the dead German soldiers who lined the streets and fields after the many battles he drove through. This armband is a constant reminder of what the power of evil can do to youth and how they can be led down a path that is not to ever be traveled again.

Mr. Libby also brought home a portrait that a German artist had painted of Charles while he was in Germany. This portrait captured a soldier in time and what he looked like as he served his great country. Another was to be painted by the same artist but time had run out for Charles there in Witzenhausen and they never had the opportunity to begin the second. This painted portrait hangs in the living room of Mr. Libby close to the chair he rests in on a daily basis. As he rises from this comfortable chair to move about his house, he sees himself captured in time over seventy years ago in a place that he remembers daily with mixed, but mostly proud emotions.

Other items include the German pistol that I spoke of previously as well as some German and French currency in a very small amount, nothing compared to that of Malvestuto. The wealth of photographs that he views on a regular basis are by far the most prized of possessions that he has as a reminder of WWII. You can often find Mr. Libby with his many albums of WWII photos at the American Legion or the VFW showing these photos to other veterans and sharing stories of his time spent in this war. All reminders and pieces of history preserved by a man that is part of the history himself. As the author, I am very excited that I have at my disposal a wealth of photo history about the stories I have written and the capturing of these images to put faces and places together.

When the American occupation drew to an end, the soldiers, including Charles, headed back to La Havre, France to prepare for the long journey home. Each soldier was flooded with their memories of the war, memories of the people that they would be leaving and certainly memories of those they left behind long ago in the United States who they would be seeing very soon. These preserved memories will either bring great joy to those who would tell them more than seventy years later or great sadness within the soldier themselves when reminded of many of these times. For Mr. Libby, the feelings are mixed but one thing is certain, he does enjoy talking about these memories and hopes that those who read or listen to them enjoy what he experienced during his time . . . *From the Command Car.*

Death in Many Forms

* * *

IN THE FIRST BOOKS OF the Bible, is mention of the Book of Life or the muster-roll of God, in which all the people who are to be considered righteous before God himself are recorded forever. God has such a book. To be blotted out of it signifies death. If some of the people of this time during WWII could have only seen this book and tried to avoid their horrible demise, many of these stories would have possibly been avoided. Death came without prejudice to the allies, axis and to non-military men and women in many forms. More than 70 million human beings were killed in WWII with many of these deaths being that of civilians from the many nations of Europe and much of the South Pacific.

Throughout the interview process, Mr. Libby makes reference to death as if it were something that he had to get used to as if it was *business as usual*. In actuality, this type of a mental defense mechanism was something that every soldier had to develop during their duty and service to this great cause for all of mankind. A displacement of emotions and a conscious division of what needed to be done and what could be digested emotionally at a later time in their lives was essential. Mr. Libby was no exception to this feeling of grief, concern and prioritizing of his personal emotions. Asking a man of Mr. Libby's age, which most of us will never see, to dig deeply into the back of his mind and relive these battles, thoughts, sights, sounds, smells and many memories that have been suppressed, is a process that demands sensitivity as well as the under standing of how to approach this writing skill as an author. With understanding the feelings of the families and the emotional strain on the man who voluntarily tells his story, I hope to somehow capture how he dealt with what he saw and how he still feels to this very day on an emotional level.

In no specific order of time, place or relevance to the events as they unfolded historically, this chapter will focus on death itself and how it was witnessed by Mr. Charles Libby from the many places that he traveled through WWII from the command car. These random comments and quotes from Mr. Libby are to the point and puts many things into the proper context of what really did happen.

OMAHA BEACH . . .

```
"When I came off the boat, there were dead
bodies all around us. They were picking them
up but couldn't pick them up fast enough.
Some of our boys were still floating in the
water. They were killed getting out of the
landing barges on the initial invasion. I
saw soldiers picking up half bodies, arms
and other bloody pieces of our guys. These
were the first dead bodies that I saw and
the first sign that I would see a lot of
death in this damn war. I saw a soldier with
half of his face blown off and immediately
turned my head forward to watch where I was
going so I wouldn't hit any of the concrete
or wooden barricades that the Germans had
placed all over the beach to try and stop
our vehicles."
```

From The Command Car

A BLOODY ROAD NEAR AACHEN, GERMANY . . .

Bodies crunching underneath the tanks and the weakened voice of a German soldier's last words, *Comrade! Comrade!* This is a memory of Mr. Libby while driving down a darkened road one evening in an area around Aachen, Germany.

A night drive for the 628th moving toward their next location prevented any stopping and visibility was limited. Knowing that Germans were in this area, the men drove right through this road running over the bodies. Some soldiers already dead and some were just barely alive. The crunching and splatting sounds are still fresh in Mr. Libby's mind and as he tells this part of the story, he verbally imitates many of these gruesome sounds which adds additional understanding for me as I write about this form of death that he personally witnessed.

```
"Their guts were coming out of their mouths
and making all kinds of sounds. Bones were
snapping like large branches of a tree. It
was a horrible thing to see and hear but I
wasn't permitted to stop. Thank God it was
dark and I couldn't see it too well. I drove
right past all of them and followed the tank
in front of me trying to forget about what
I was witnessing and hearing at the time.
We all hoped that it was only German bodies
and that none of them were Americans. It was
just awful!"
```

IN NO SPECIFIC PLACE DURING THE WAR, BUT EVERYWHERE AROUND US . . .

```
"I heard screams of dying soldiers and hands
flailing in the air as I drove past them
```

watching the medics take our boys away. They dealt with a lot of death and did their jobs well. Every now and then we would help load the GI's if we were stopped, but mostly I witnessed the medics from the rear echelon do most of the dirty, bloody work."

DEAD GERMAN SOLDIERS WERE EVERYWHERE...

"I saw dead Germans everywhere! For some reason, I didn't get as sad to see *them* all over the place. It wasn't that I was an animal, I just knew that they were there to kill us so it just didn't bother me quite as much as *our* seeing boys dead. I would prop them up along the road, the Germans, then I would search their pockets for documents or I would drag them out of the way for vehicles to get through, and all the while it never bothered me."

Buchenwald Concentration Camp in Weimar, Germany finishes out this particularly sad chapter of this manuscript. For Mr. Libby, the memories of this camp offer a suggestion as to the limits that he had for himself mentally and spiritually. As much as it was business as usual, this camp drew a hard line as to what he really wanted to see and experience as a soldier, as a man and most of all, as a Christian.

The duty of liberating this death camp came during this late period of occupation. Word had started to spread down the lines about these types of camps toward the end of the fighting. Mr. Libby couldn't remember any talk of them in the early months and even throughout the first year of his time spent in Europe.

He commented that they kept them secret, even from their own citizens and the only time that they heard of them is when they were getting placed in the camp themselves!

C-Company moved in a large truck traveling to this camp to help out in any way they could lend a hand. Mr. Libby chose *not* to go and see all the death. This particluar mission was a voluntary duty trip that wasn't required for everyone in the unit. The men in the unit asked if Charles wanted to go with them and he quickly refused.

> "I just didn't want to see all the things that they were telling us happened there and I had already seen enough death during this war. It just wasn't for me."

As the soldiers returned to their bivouac area, they told Charles what they had seen. I can see in the eyes of Mr. Libby his sadness for the people who suffered there. I can also see that even though he didn't step foot into the camp, he can still remember the smell of death in the air that surrounded his own camp. He can also remember the photos that they gave to him that he later destroyed and I can see that he looks deep within his own soul to find a reason for the senseless deaths that happened there and in the many other concentration camps that were spread throughout the country.

> "When the guys got back to camp, they told me about all that they had seen. It sounded horrible! The only thing that I missed was that all the high ranking American generals were there as well as some of the other allied commanders. I really wish that I had gone just for that reason, to see and possibly meet all of them in one place that day."

Some of the memories of the stories told from the other GI's included the awful smell in the air. The piles of bodies described to Mr. Libby were much like what was present after a snow plow would clear the roads back home in Pennsylvania. The showers had scratches on the walls complete with finger nails remaining in them. Piles of their personal articles and everything under the sun were all organized and as high as any of the soldiers that were there taking care of the few remaining survivors.

Survivors were like walking skeletons with just skin covering their bones. Some were so weak from malnutrition that they had to be loaded onto stretchers to be taken out of the camp. Others weren't so lucky and died right there in front of our guys before they could be helped. Bodies of Jews lined the camp and were treated by the Nazi's like trophies or symbols of their might and power. The thought that they were inferior to the Germans gave them a guilt-free attempt to cleanse their country of this race of beloved people.

Upon arrival at the camp, the soldiers who entered it's gates read a sign that hung over the entryway which read *"Jedam das Seine."* The literal German translation of this slogan or saying was *"to each his own."* The slang version of this horrible saying translated as *"everyone gets what he deserves."* This said it all! This is why people like Mr. Charles A. Libby went to war and all the others who sacrificed their time and many, their lives. Death came in many forms but this was the type of death that to this day is still completely unbelievable to all mankind. God rest all that suffered and died there and may they rest in peace forever in his kingdom!

Home Sweet Home

✳ ✳ ✳

IF YOUR HAIR STARTS FALLING out from stress, you know that whatever you are doing or whatever you had done was something extraordinarily stressful and something that you wouldn't *ever* want to repeat. That's just what happened to Charles Libby upon his return to the shores of the United States, in clumps, his hair was coming out at the roots.

> "When I finally got back into Williamsport, PA my doctor told me that my nerves weren't settled down yet from what I went through and that was what was causing my hair to fall out in small patches. It took nearly three months for my hair to stop falling out and to grow back in the way it was."

His return home with his fellow tank destroyers wasn't filled with the fanfare or the return celebrations along with the others of his unit. An unfortunate accident kept him there in Germany a bit longer than the others shipping out as they returned to the United States. After washing his blankets in gasoline to rid them of germs which were causing a rash on his body, he had poured a five gallon can into a large container which unknowingly contained hot ashes. The flash caused burns on both his face and both of his arms. Running from the flames, Charles's arms were still on fire. To put the flames out, he placed them between his legs and in doing so, peeled all of the skin off. For many weeks to come, Charles had to painfully rub Vaseline ointment on the burns to help the slow and painful healing process.

> "They took me sixty miles down the road in a jeep with just a towel over my arms. No purple heart for this type of injury. I had second and third degree burns all over my arms and it hurt really bad!"

For over three weeks, Charles stayed in a hospital there in Belgium where the accident had occurred. This was not only a long and painful reminder to Charles as to his serious accident but a painful reminder of how it put him that much further from going home with the rest of the GI's from his company which made this emotionally painful. He painfully served three months of additional work there with the army as a switchboard operator in Heiligenstadt, Germany until the next transport boat would leave with the second wave of soldiers that would be ready to go home after their allotted time spent in combat.

> "One day two MP's came into the switchboard communications center and asked me if I knew this girl that they had with them. She had a butcher knife and wanted to kill a girl that I had been seeing for a short time. I guess this Polish girl loved me and wanted me for herself. I told them to take her outside and take her back home. That was really a close one. I just wanted to get home in one piece!"

One more broken heart before the trip home and another memory from the mind of a soldier who once again was protected by a letter he carried and a strong belief in God.

The American ship would leave with these soldiers from La Havre, France and the voyage would drop all of these war heroes at the port in Boston, Massachusetts. Elmer Knopf came into the switchboard communications center and told Charles that he and his buddies were to get their things packed up.

> "Elmer told me, Charlie, you're going home! Pack your stuff and get ready to ship out."

These were the words that Charles waited to hear all of these long months in battle. Although there were many enjoyable moments and the experiences that he learned from and would take into his adult life that were beneficial, it was certainly time to get back home. The men were all told that they could only have one pistol and one pair field glasses to take home.

> "I thought, well I made it through the war, I burned my arms, but I made it out alive. It was time to pack up my stuff and I still think about the items that I had to leave there so that I wouldn't get into trouble. I had pearl-handled pistols and other weapons that I could have brought home with me. Then, they didn't even check us as we got onto the boat! That really made me mad."

The men did what they were told and were ready for the long voyage back home. The US military had converted over three-hundred cargo vessels into transports which were used for the job of returning United States soldiers back home as well as the injured and the now freed POW's. Mr. Libby comments on this trip with a big laugh and an even bigger smile on his face.

> "It took a while to get a ship to bring us home due to a ship strike back in the US. It was sea sickness for most of the returning

> soldiers all over again! Elmer Knopf and I had the dinner table to ourselves while we were eating. I asked him to pass the milk and he said just wait a minute and it will be there. He no sooner said it and it slid down to me due to the swaying of the ship."

On the second night of this journey back to the United States, an announcement was made to the men aboard the vessel that it had been reported by HQ back in France that a piece of US military equipment had come up missing and it was believed that it was on board illegally. This US issued army property turned out to be a weapon that was highly sought after by soldiers as a souvenir to bring home to the US.

An air-cooled .30 caliber machine gun was the prize that was missing and possibly on board the ship. These guns were a new addition to the American military arsenal. In WWI, water cooled machine guns were used by the American soldiers. Introduced in WWII, the air-cooled guns replaced the older models and performed much better in battle. The announcement to the men was stern and to the point.

> "They told us over the loud speaker that a machine gun was missing and it was believed that it was brought on board in a soldier's duffel bag. They announced that if they didn't find the gun that *nobody* was getting off of the boat when we reached Boston. We all knew that they meant it but nobody wanted to get involved. But, it took care of itself later that night."

That night, the demands and possible consequences that would befall these men caused enough concern to produce the requested results in its recovery. It came to pass that a soldier had indeed taken this particular weapon to bring home and decided that it was not worth any type of penalty and gave it up in the darkness of night while the men on board the ship were sleeping.

> "The next morning, the gun was found on the kitchen cutting board. It was fully assembled and sitting there for the cook to find and turn in to the commander. He must have brought it on board disassembled or it wouldn't have fit in his duffel bag. We were all relieved that it turned up and didn't have to stay on the ship after our long journey to *finally* get home."

Upon arrival in Boston, the soldiers had a small celebration of cheering and appreciation for being back in the United States. Soldiers were yelling "*We're back in the US!* and *It's good to be home!*" rang throughout the ship. A train would be their next form of transportation back to Indiantown Gap, PA to serve there until they had fulfilled their required military service time. A little guard duty, military drills and other redundant chores on the base filled their time along with a little gambling between the GI's in the form of dice games like craps. Anything to keep their sanity while they waited for these final few days to get home to their families.

As a curious writer as well as a lover of American history, I wondered during these interviews if Mr. Libby had ever seen German soldiers or personally met them after the war was over and what transpired during any of these meetings. I personally wondered what the feeling would be after your mindset was to kill them on sight or be killed yourself. After asking the question to Mr. Libby, he responded with this short story.

After debarking the ship, the men filed into a large gymnasium which was set up with long tables and a prepared hot meal for the soldiers. It was a shocking moment for Charles to see that they were about to be served by *Germans* who had immigrated to the United States and were now working as civilians for the United States Army there at the military base in Pennsylvania.

> "A German serving all of us at our table wanted to talk to us. He spoke in broken English and told us that he loved America and told us how beautiful the country was. They had a lot of respect for us and what we had done. They gave us a great meal which was better than the meal I got in England before I left there and didn't have to worry if it was poisoned."

These men that served the soldiers were prisoners of war and got a second chance in life to enjoy the freedoms that we as Americans may overlook each day. Mr. Libby indicted that the war was over and that the men were courteous and grateful for this chance. He also said that to hold a grudge or to be disrespectful didn't set well with him and that it was time to move forward and forgive them.

One evening at the base, shortly after their return home, the soldiers all gathered in the activity room to watch an Errol Flynn movie entitled *Sheepherder*. After the film was over, an officer who was seated in the front row stood up to address all of these returning soldiers.

> "He asked all of us if anyone wanted to re-enlist. He offered all of us three months vacation and two-hundred and fifty dollars if we wanted to re-up. If we wanted to stay in the outfit, we were supposed to stay in the room and if we didn't want to, we could leave. Only one guy stayed in the room and

> the rest of us all got up and left. We had seen and done enough and my time was certainly over in the army. I was ready to get back home to my family. I served proudly and did what I thought I was supposed to do, but *no more for me!*"

Officially on November 18th of 1945, Charles A. Libby of C-Company within the 628th Tank Destroyer Battalion with the grade of T5 was Honorably Discharged from his military service for the United States of America! His separation station was the same place where he began his initial service in Indiantown Gap, Pennsylvania and his next destination was to be his old home in Williamsport!

Approximately six months of service here in the states was all that Charles Libby was shy to fulfill his sworn obligations to Uncle Sam's Army. A passenger train that was supposed to take this command car driver home to his family had already left for Williamsport and the next one wouldn't be leaving for several more hours. Charles was used to enduring and things going as planned, so like so many times before in Europe, he took measures into his own hands.

> "I didn't want to wait for the next train, I wanted to go home! So, I asked the rail attendant if he would make sure that my duffel bag would get onto the late train to Williamsport. He agreed and said that he would take care of it for a soldier. I hitched a ride as far as Sunbury, PA and my sister came and picked me up from there and took me back home."

Upon arriving home, Charles's mother came quickly down the porch steps to greet her returning son. There were plenty of hugs for Charles and even more thanks to God for returning him home safely. Her pride and joy was home again and her worst worries were finally settled. The power of prayer from a faithful mother and the *Letter of Protection* that Charles brought home with him after carrying it across the continent of Europe, as well as the skillful way Charles handled himself throughout every battle he faced, says it all.

As Mr. Libby talks about that particular moment in time upon his return, it is very brief with little words, followed by a long pause as if he is once again looking at the mental snapshot that he took in his mind of his mother's face as he saw her love for him as they embraced. He fights back the tears with a hard swallow and a smile for his mother that only a son can display. Mr. Libby knew how much she loved and cared for him. He knew the absolute *hell* she must have felt day in and day out while she heard reports on the radio of the many battles as well as hearing of soldiers being killed in action. He struggled with the mixed feelings of his great pride as well as guilt in causing these emotions for his beloved mother. But with a hug, the look into his eyes, her words of thanks to God and smiles all around, it was finally over! The worries can now disappear, the long days and nights of feeling helpless and the hardships of not having her son there who was such an important part of aiding the Libby family in any way he could were now over. A faithful woman and her faithful son – reunited at last!

```
"I wasn't too good at writing letters so I
only sent a few home to let her know that I
was alright and alive. She was really glad
to finally see me there alive and standing
right there in front of her."
```

Life was finally going to get back to normal, with some added benefits of course. Nobody shooting burp guns at him, no need to sleep with one eye open or wake up with three inches of snow on top of him, no ducking for cover under his command car to avoid an air burst and certainly no need to wonder if he would be the one that day that medics would carry on a stretcher to the rear echelon of his unit covered in his own blood in a body bag.

When going out into the public, Charles was very proud to wear his US Army uniform. People he would see and speak to appreciated what he had done in serving his country and not only showed him more respect, but thanked him for what he had done in Europe which affected them back here in the United States of America!

```
"When people saw those patches that I had
on my sleeves, they knew who I was with and
what I had done! My father and mother were
very proud of me and that made me feel very
good. It also made me feel like I was fi-
nally appreciated and that they now thought
of me as a man!"
```

There was so much to do and so much to see for Charles. He was finally home and in his mind, had a lot of catching up to do. To taste the food he grew up eating, to see the beautiful sights he longed to see and to visit some of the important people in his life that he missed while he was away for what may have seemed like an eternity. But first on this laundry list of personal desires was to visit the author of the Dear John letter he received one day as the supply truck arrived with mail from home while under fire from Germans in Belgium. It was time for a visit to the woman that he loved and who caused him great pain, confusion and sorrow while so far away from home serving his country.

Earline lived nearby and without hesitation, the desire to see her face-to-face was overwhelming for Charles to say the least. At the time of receiving the letter, he made quick and responsible thought of dismissing the bad news and to personally deal with it later when he would return home to the states. The thoughts of this reunion of sorts, flooded his mind on the boat trip back to US shores and now the time was here to finally face her and see how she would react to his return and what she had to say to him in person.

The knock on the door was answered by Earline herself. With a surprised look on her face from both guilt and seeing this handsome uniformed GI standing at her door, the two looked at each other for a brief moment without words. Charles said, *hello Earline* and she returned the greeting with, *hello Charles*.

Charles was invited into her home to find that she was hosting a couple's card party. Among the guests were three couples seated together and one gentleman who was apparently unaccompanied. Charles immediately figured that the single man must be her new love. Charles was politely introduced to each of the guests as well as the man that had replaced his seat in the card games.

```
"I was very courteous and didn't try to
start anything. I just wanted for her to see
me and what I had become while I was away
fighting in a war. I have to be honest; I
also wanted her to feel a little guilty that
she hadn't stayed faithful to me while I was
over there. I fooled around a little with
girls over there but only after her letter
came to me. I knew it was over between us
but still wanted her to know that I was back
home again and safe."
```

The two saw one another from time to time and remained friends. Charles moved into the world of dating as a man who had stories to earn respect as well as the stories that would catch the interest of the many interested, single women of his small hometown. The uniform helped him as well being an attractive tool to strike up a conversation.

The *home sweet home* attitude continued for Charles and his life would be filled with many challenges that he would now face as a man with experiences from which he could draw from. Any challenge that he faced would be considered to be minor compared to the problem solving he faced as a soldier who was performing his duty . . . *From the Command Car.*

The Men Who Fought

* * *

THE 628TH TANK DESTROYER UNIT was a fighting force that proudly claims to have been the greatest fighting force of the entire war. Their military might was proven during their many battles they faced throughout the entire war while fighting in the European Theater. American and foreign citations for the 628th and C-Company alike, solidified their status as great warriors. But, without the attached units that had their own specialized duties and forms of fighting, the 628th would had been limited within their specialized fighting capabilities.

To not mention these additional units that were attached to this tank destroyer unit would leave a large piece of the *victory puzzle* missing. To also honor those who he fought with and saw at their side, day in and day out, Mr. Libby would like to make mention of these particular units, foreign friends, officers and enlisted men and give them their deserved credit for their abilities and acts of heroism.

One mention as to beginning this particular chapter was made by Mr. Libby about the men themselves who he would like to give their due credits.

```
"I didn't get to learn everyone's names be-
cause we always moved to fast. They had a
job to do and did as well. We weren't all
together for too long, just in passing most
of the time except the men that I was next
```

> to in my car day after day. They all did a fine job and were all very brave soldiers."

Mr. Libby starts this heart-filled, yet simple tribute to the following who he respects and misses very, very much.

SPECIAL THANKS TO THE FOLLOWING COMPANIES ...
A-Company, B-Company, C-Company, Reconnaissance Company, 82nd Airborne, 101st Airborne, 5th Armored Division and General Patton's 3rd Armored Division.

SPECIAL THANKS TO OUR FOREIGN FIGHTING FRIENDS ...
The Canadians, The French Guerrilla Fighters and The British Commandos.

SPECIAL THANKS TO THE FOLLOWING OFFICERS ...
Lt. Colonel William Gallagher, Captain Robert Jones, Colonel John Tupper Cole, Sergeant Isaac Luckey, Sergeant Charles Leo, Sergeant Ernest Kirschbaum and Sergeant Joseph Drost.

SPECIAL THANKS TO MY ENLISTED BUDDIES ...
Edward Bik, Robert "Pete" Peterson, Marvin Phillips, Jim Luvender, Joseph Malvestuto and Elmer Knopf and to all the boys that also served in the CCC Camps that also joined the military.

> "Thanks to all of the guys who saved my butt countless times over! I made it home, some of you didn't and for that I am forever saddened and grateful. May we all meet again one day in a much better place where there

are no wars or fighting. I also hope that if there are any of my personal buddies from that time who are still alive and see this, that they contact me to meet one last time and share memories from what seems to be an entirely separate life than what we now live. God Bless all of you!"

Later in Life

✳ ✳ ✳

As I proof the lines of this manuscript with Mr. Libby and read the words that he had spoken to me in our countless meetings, interviews and telephone calls, an overwhelming rush of emotions and urgency flow from his very being. From a big smile of happiness or pride to a steady flow of tears capturing the emotions of loss, sorrow, family and days gone by. To hear your life being spoken to you by another is a bitter-sweet experience to say the least. I too feel his many emotions as they become written as clearly on his face as the words appear on the paper in front of me from which I read. A part of a generation of men who served in this war had either died somewhere over there or had come back home to the US to live a full life and later pass on without ever having their story properly recorded for others to hear, enjoy and more importantly, to learn from.

This great opportunity that was presented to me on behalf of Mr. Libby has to be one of the biggest highlights of my life and for this I am forever grateful. I sometimes find myself rushing to get as much done for Mr. Libby's sake as he enjoys the ripe old age of 97 and try my hardest to become inspired to write all day long and late into the night. I also feel an obligation to everyone that served in war during these times and slow myself down to make sure that I capture the element of the many emotions as well as properly relay the truths that were spoken to me. All-in-all, a project of this undertaking is a great burden as well as an enjoyable form of artistic expression for me.

I know the man Mr. Libby better now as he speaks to me and has over the past seven years. In both his stories and in his private words, I can see the man he is and was as well as the boy he remembers himself as. A truly blessed man to be able to tell a wonderful story as well as completely enthrall you into the time or situation as if you were right there living it and seeing it first-hand. A stern man when it comes to telling the story properly and slightly impatient when we get side-tracked or when time starts to slip away from us. He has preserved these memories and wishes for them to be a *learning tool* to help prevent anything like this from ever happening again, so time is most certainly of great importance.

I would also like to add that Mr. Libby is a man that is still very much full of life and enthusiasm. As I travel with him to the many speeches that we give at libraries, churches and nursing homes alike, everyone is in shock to know his current age as well as how active he still is and the activities that he still participates in with a youthful vigor. He is truly an inspiration to many and a wealth of information that he feely shares with whoever wishes to listen.

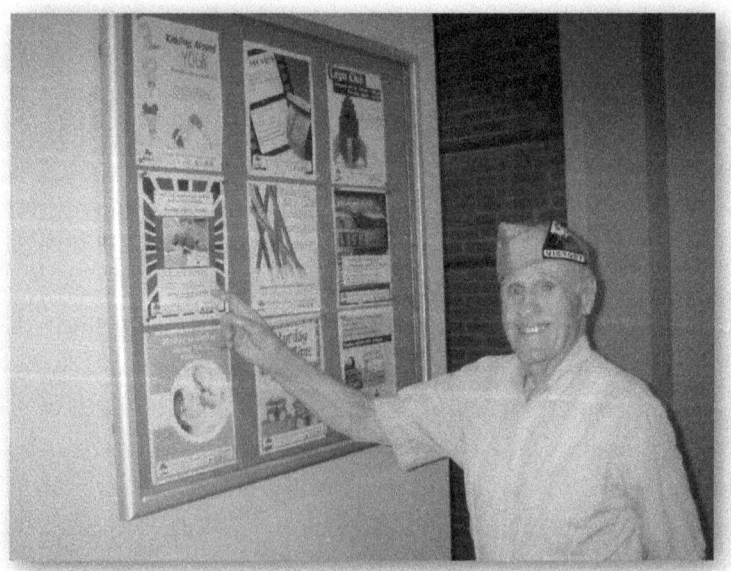

Mr. Charles Libby at The Union County Library admiring an advertisement for our joint speech.

Also a matter of interest, I have chosen to give a few details of the life of this WWII veteran and hero at the conclusion of this manuscript for those who would be interested in what his life was like between the years after the war and of his life here in the now. I would make the assumption that many of this younger generation in *the now* who read this will also enjoy hearing of the simple yet fulfilling life a soldier lives after what they would think of as exciting. You see, the journey is actually the reward and the experiences that life itself provides for you each day are it's true blessings. In the long life of Mr. Charles Ardell Libby, there have been many ups and downs and I have chosen to document a few details to show the events that are considered to be in the *ups* category.

For the former command car driver of the 628th, it was back home to the small town of Williamsport, Pennsylvania and the great task began to find a job or a type of career for the man that went to war as a boy and came back a man with new responsibilities and entirely new set of priorities.

There were many small jobs here and there to make ends meet and continue to help his family until the opportunity was presented to Charles to start his very own garbage route in the area that he lived. This became over a twenty year career for Mr. Libby and provided a home and educations for his children and an ability to provide the most basic of needs for his new wife Virginia and his growing family. For Mr. Libby, the hard work of this route was a welcomed change from mortars and bullets whizzing past his head and enduring the frigid temperatures of Europe while sleeping under the stars at night without any type of roof or protection from Mother Nature. Instead of picking up the remains of dead American soldiers, he now picked up the trash from American families that enjoy the very freedom to buy, eat or consume whatever they wanted.

```
"I liked my garbage route. I made good money
and enjoyed talking to all the people on my
route as well. I would be given stuff that
```

> was still good and would take it home with me. In the fall I would have a big sale and make good money selling all that I didn't keep for myself."

A similar type of mind-set of the soldier that found many ways to make extra money while in the European Theater as well as always finding a way to provide for those around him.

Charles Libby married in the early fifties and shortly after that, started a family. Starting a family was an easy thing for this soft hearted man who knew how important family was to have happiness in life itself. Fathering four children, three are still living and doing well with terrific careers and live according to their Christian faith. One child passed away in the fifties after a respiratory illness which still to this day causes sadness to Mr. Libby. But, as life takes its turns and winds along the path of experiences, the blessings outweigh the bad times by far.

The 628th Tank Destroyer Unit held reunions periodically throughout the years. Mr. Libby was always both honored and excited to attend these gatherings to see his old war buddies and to share the stories once again from the battlefields of Europe as well as the newer stories from here in the United States about their careers and their new families. Not dawning their uniforms, but wearing civilian clothes just as men with a very similar and connecting past and the many stories to share with one another.

A very special memory occurred while attending one of these 628th reunions. When in an elevator with his wife, a moment alone with Lt. Colonel Gallagher made Mr. Libby very proud.

> "Lt. Colonel Gallagher spoke to my wife and told her, I always liked Libby and he was a good soldier. He told her that I always looked like a gentleman and acted the way a

```
soldier should act. I was very happy to hear
him say that."
```

These simple words still ring in the ears of Mr. Libby as being the *seal of approval* that he wanted to achieve as a soldier. To be trusted and to make his commander happy was enough for Charles Libby to be proud of what he had done. His eyes still start to well up with tears as he tells the story of that moment with great pride and respect for the commander that he looked up to while in combat.

While in the hospitality room at this hotel where the 628th reunion was held, Mr. Libby remembers hearing all the exciting stories from his GI buddies. When they first started the reunions, up to two-hundred and fifty men attended and it seemed as if it was something that would happen regularly. Later in the years of trying to organize these reunions, only fourteen attended the final 628th reunion and through a show of hands vote, these precious reunions were dissolved and communication between these soldiers would be more random with stories and reports of the others from the unit passing on and the stories of these men to only be found in the obituary pages of newspapers and in the photos in albums of those who remember these great men of the 628th Tank Destroyer Battalion.

At the final reunion which Lt. Colonel Gallagher attended in West Middlesex, Pennsylvania, he proudly provided a written letter to the men in attendance from headquarters. This document was in reference to a citation that the 628th Tank Destroyer Battalion had received from the government of France. This particular bit of information made each and every one of these men very proud and it is Mr. Libby's wish to have this documentation known. It reads as such . . .

HEADQUARTERS
628th Tank Destroyer Battalion Reunion
West Middlesex, Penna.

The following information has been provided by Brig. Gen. Robert M. Gaynor, DSC, first commander of Company C, 628th TD as a result of his research in the Army Archives: General Orders No. 24, Department of the Army, Washington, D.C., 10 December 1947, page 86, states that the 628th Tank Destroyer Battalion, attached to Combat Command R, 5th Armored Division was awarded:

THE FRENCH CROIX DE GUERRE WITH SILVER STAR

In accordance with decision No. 246, 15 July 1946, by the President of the Provisional Government of the French Republic.

<u>CITATION</u>

"A group of units, inspired by a fierce will to conquer. It especially distinguished itself in the breakthrough of the Siegfried Line in Wallendorf, Germany. From the 14th to the 20th of September 1944, it threw itself into the attack on the city and drove the enemy from it. It continued its advance and seized a bridge over the river Oure. Subject to a counterattack, supported by tanks, and in spite of heavy losses, Combat Command R and its attached 628th Tank Destroyer Battalion, never-the-less continued its advance, penetrating farther and farther into Germany."

10-11-12 July 1981

And the document was signed at the bottom saying . . .

"1 World's Best!"   Bill Gallagher

Mr. Charles Libby and Lt. Colonel Gallagher at one of the last 628th Reunions.

This special award showed the men that what they had done was appreciated by the people that they did it for. Their sacrifices and their hard work was something that helped many for generations to come. Mr. Libby and his attending tank mates were recognized and forever sealed in history as being tough, brave, loved and most of all, greatly appreciated!

When I asked if Mr. Libby had been back to the places he fought during those years spent in WWII, he solemnly commented as such.

"I really wanted to go back to France and Germany and some of the other places that I fought in during the official anniversary celebrations throughout the years but my garbage route and my family were more important at the time. I had a wonderful wife and children that needed me. I really wish that I could have gone to see what it looked like now after the war. I watched some of the events on television and it hurt me that I couldn't go over and be with some of my buddies who were there."

When asked if he would like to still go now in his advanced age, he comments as such.

"I'd really love to go back there someday soon! Especially to Luxemburg where I heard there was a monument to the 628th Tank Destroyer Unit for liberating them. An old friend from A-Company went there and carried his discharge papers with him on the trip. A man read them to the crowd near the monument and he said that the more he read, the louder the crowd got with their cheering for this soldier of the 628th. I would also like to see if any of the women that I used to dance with were still alive and thank them for all of the great times we had together."

The words of a man up in his years and the desire to travel back to the place that provided so many memories for all these years puts life into a perspective of capturing the moments when you have the chance and never allowing time to get away from you without fulfilling your deepest dreams. Enjoy the journey!

As one part of his journey in life, Mr. Libby and his family started a family restaurant in the Williamsport area called *The Rax*. This was a collective effort between he and his sons and was opened for business nearly nine years with a good reputation and most of all, great food!

One regular customer was a man that worked for the Office of Veterans Administration. He had asked Charles about the war and his unit. After the many stories from Mr. Libby of his service and where he had been, the man asked him about his medals. Mr. Libby surprised the man by telling him that he didn't receive any medals or citations for his service in WWII.

```
"The guy told me, Charlie you have a bunch
of medals that you were supposed to get. I
told him that I didn't think that I was sup-
posed to get any. I was there to do my job
for my country and I did it. That was it in
my mind."
```

After investigation by the VA representative, the proper report was filed for the necessary medals that Mr. Libby was entitled to upon his late return home to the states. Arriving back home after his fellow C-Company brothers created some confusion and the presentation of these medals was never executed and the man that had served so bravely never had the chance to experience the appreciation and fanfare that he so deserved.

It took almost a year of waiting, but the man came through for Mr. Charles A. Libby and gave him his medals that he truly deserved. There were no crowds around to see it, there was no confetti and there was no high officer pinning these medals on his uniform. A simple handing over of these prized symbols of his achievements at the counter of a restaurant. This pretty much rings true as to the type of soldier that Charles was all through his service in WWII. No flash, no trying to steal the spotlight, just hard work and a simple thank you was all that he ever expected.

Today, Mr. Libby is indeed very proud of his many medals and service badges from WWII and keeps them safely displayed behind the glass of two shadow boxes, never wearing them on his uniform that he dawns from time to time for very special and formal occasions or speeches that he is asked to give to interested listeners. As the author of this book, I thought it only fitting to celebrate the great accomplishments of Mr. Charles A. Libby by listing his medals and what the US military requirements are for receiving each one of these prized awards.

Mr. Charles A. Libby has received the following medals and badges for his service in WWII :

European African Middle-Eastern Campaign Medal with 4 Bronze Stars
This particular medal was presented to Mr. Libby for his participation in the European theater during WWII and he is permitted to wear the 4 bronze service stars on the medal itself.

Good Conduct Medal
This particular medal was presented to Mr. Libby for more than three consecutive years of "honorable and faithful" service without any form of non-judicial punishment, disciplinary infractions or court martial offenses. It is one of the oldest military medals and the one that makes Mr. Libby the most proud.

Honorable Service Medal
This particular medal was presented to Mr. Libby for his honorable service and sacrifices during time spent in WWII.

VICTORY MEDAL WWII
This particular medal was presented to Mr. Libby for his active duty in Europe during WWII during the appropriate time frame of the final allied victory.

ARMY OF OCCUPATION WWII MEDAL
This particular medal was presented to Mr. Libby for recognition of his service during the occupation period in Germany for which he performed his duties with honor.

AMERICAN DEFENSE SERVICE MEDAL
This particular medal was presented to Mr. Libby for his service before America's entry into WWII during the initial years of the European conflict.

AMERICAN CAMPAIGN MEDAL
This particular medal was presented to Mr. Libby for his service performed in the American Theater of Operations during WWII.

SUB-MACHINE GUN BADGE
This particular badge was presented to Mr. Libby for his skillful qualification of becoming a sharpshooter on the military shooting range.

Of course, a rating of T5, Tech Sergeant, is also another of this soldier's personal accomplishments. This was a man who had to leave school in the eighth grade to help his family during their struggles. This was a man with a limited education who had a spirit that wouldn't quit. These accomplishments are extraordinary and show how determination and hard work can help you to accomplish great things in life!

Mr. Libby's wife and mother to his children of many years passed away leaving Charles to be there for his children alone. He remembers her fondly and a tear of sadness comes into his eye as he speaks of her and a hint of the feeling that he wished she could have been near him as he recited the stories of this manuscript. He chose not to relive those particular memories by telling of her passing by just saying that she was a good woman and that he will see her again in Heaven someday soon. He remains a single man who comments this about ever finding another wife or girlfriend at the age of 97.

> "Many women have asked me, Charlie, why don't you go steady with just one girl? I tell them that I am too old to have just one girlfriend or to marry again. I am having too much fun dancing with whoever I want to when I go out and I dance with a lot of them!"

Dancing is the great joy within the very being of Mr. Libby. Dancing with the young girls of the day and improving his skills, Charles spent time at The Park Ballroom and any other place that offered the music he loved so much and the many available women to dance with. And to this very day, he spends several hours a week attending dances at American Legion Posts, VFW halls, Moose Club and other organizations that give these soldiers and dancers alike, a place to practice and enjoy their passion.

> "I have several dance partners who can really dance! When I get out on the floor with one of them that can dance really well, all the people stop and watch us and tell us how good we look together out on the dance floor."

As I myself go to watch him dance and see if it is just the bragging of an old GI and tank man, I found that he is still very talented as a dancer and that he does captivate those who enjoy watching him glide across the floor with his partner even at the age of 97! A waltz, a ch-cha or standing in front of his partner and dancing a more modern style of dance, he truly enjoys this form of entertainment, exercise, interaction and the many songs that bring back the memories of his time behind the wheel *from the command car.*

On another note about the blessed and exciting life of this WWII veteran, out of curiosity, I asked Mr. Libby once again about the woman who sent him the Dear John letter long ago during the war. A final note in the chapter of this turbulent relationship with a girl he once loved came into his sharp mind.

```
"Many years ago, I heard that Earline was on
her death bed in the hospital. I struggled
with whether I should go and see her or not.
My sons told me that I shouldn't go because
of what she did years ago, but I decided that
I should go and see her one last time out of
respect. We used to have something special
a long time ago and I thought it would be
proper to at least tell her goodbye."
```

Mr. Libby did just that. He visited her as she lay in her bed during her final moments. When she saw Charles enter the room, she looked into his eyes and smiled. Mr. Libby commented to me that she didn't look good and he knew that her time was nearing the end. He walked to the bed and told her that he was sorry that she was there and sad that she wasn't doing well. She looked at him and told him that she was dying. The two spent time together in the room speaking one final time. When it was time for Mr. Libby to leave her, he leaned over her, kissed her on the cheek and with a soft *God Bless*, told her goodbye one last time and walked out of the hospital room, ending any bitterness from the past with only the memory of this sweet encounter and final goodbye.

More recently, Mr. Libby was invited to be the Grand Marshall at a local parade. The extreme pride and joy of sitting in the lead car and the relief that he wasn't the one having to drive a more important man himself, was a highlight of his life. To be the one that people were clapping for, saluting and taking pictures of, was a moment that will always make him a proud soldier.

The thoughts and memories of human beings flood their minds and make them who they are today. Memories of happenings both good and bad form a strong desire to either shut them out completely or a longing to go back in time and relive the relevance of those special moments. To Mr. Charles A. Libby, the feelings are that of both sides of the coin. With his strong words and emotions I can see the overwhelming desire to shut out the sights and smells of death, the knowledge of what German deaths camps held and the words which ring in his ears of his fellow C-Company GI's being labeled as KIA. With his final days on this earth approaching, I can also see his longing desires to see the beautiful sights of Europe and to visit the people who may still be living. The people that either touched his heart or gave him pleasure during a war that took a young boy from the mountains of central Pennsylvania and helped to turn him into a strong and confident man.

I would imagine that this story rings true within many of the last known, living soldiers of WWII. The understanding of what these men endured and what these men fought for as a cause and purpose is to understand how the world is shaped by events that unfold in front of us on a daily basis. As we capture images in a photograph to preserve happenings and memories, our mind reflects back to those moments of great joy or great sorrow. As we live today, be reminded to take a mental snapshot of what you are seeing around you and compare it to the evil that our soldiers saw. Use these images, stories and memories to continue to learn from our history in an effort to make the future a better place for *all* mankind. God bless each one of you, and may his promises bring you happiness and fulfillment in life and always keep you safe.

When you lay your head down to sleep tonight, be sure to thank those who have fought and are still away fighting for what is right. Be sure to thank the

Lord for the soldiers that gave so much and be sure to ask for protection for the men and women on the ground, in the air, out at sea or making their way down a dark and lonely road behind the wheel . . .

From the Command Car.

Two WWII Veterans Meet

* * *

THE RARE OPPORTUNITY TO BE able to either meet, speak or spend significant time hearing the stories of *any* living WWII hero is a memory that will never leave you. I have had many of these experiences in my adult life that I remember well. When I see an older gentleman with a service baseball cap or in my travels someone announces that he was a WWII veteran, I make sure to stop everything that I am doing to have a seat to ask if they would like to share a story or two with me and tell me whatever they would like to share. Most of the time I ask initially what theater of operations he served in and I *always* make sure to say "T*hank you very much* for your service!"

There are also rare opportunities that present themselves that are even more special and place you in what seems like a travel back in time to hear the memories of certain individuals who did something extraordinary. I was fortunate to have had one of these rare experiences during the writing of this book. Close friends, Steve and Sherry Kurtz, were friends with a man that they told me was also a WWII veteran. When mentioning him in conversation, they relayed to me that he not only had many stories that were worth hearing, but that he was someone of importance and it had something to do with D-Day. My interest peaked and I asked them if they could speak to him and allow me to call and set up some private time to go and meet with him and take Mr. Libby along to watch them interact and share stories with one another. He was very receptive and the meeting was arranged. Armed with notes and a video camera,

I took Mr. Libby to meet this fellow WWII veteran without knowing exactly what part of the *missing puzzle* he actually filled.

A trip to pick up Mr. Libby and a short drive only about 3 miles from his own home, led us to the home of Mr. Charles Missigman. A knock on the door, answered by a gray-haired man, followed by a three hour visit ensued in a private setting in his bedroom which he had made into a type of shrine focused on his time spent in the war. Mr. Libby took a seat on a couch, Mr. Missigman took his place at the foot of his bed and I on the floor behind the tripod as I asked permission to video tape the conversations for historical content. Introductions all around led us to understanding just who we have come upon and just what missing puzzle piece of the war we were spending time with. Mr. Missigman was the coroner who was in charge of processing the bodies of the men who came back from Normady, France at Omaha Beach after the invasion on *D-DAY!* This particular job was one of an unsung hero who had the arduous job of identifying and in many instances, piecing the boys back together. As we sat and listened to his stories of WWII and his time spent in France, I could not help to tear up and clear my throat as I was taken back there by a man that saw as much death as *any one man* during this particular conflict. This man freely spoke to us about what he had seen, who he was in direct communications with and what his duty was for our men that gave *everything* during those days of the initial invasions.

```
"Sometimes all we had was a finger handed
to us in a bloody cloth. They brought us ev-
ery body part imaginable and it was our job
to put them back together again. After the
third day of this, I called the president
and told him that we just could not do it
the way they wanted it done! There were just
too many of them, too quickly! We even had
to stop using body bags because we had so
```

```
      much to do with the ID process and making
      them look like a person again to ship them
      home to their loved ones. Sometimes that
      finger was all they would get in a small box
      for the funeral."
```

Now, I was so used to hearing Mr. Libby tell one story after another with no interuption or a chance of even thinking about interupting him, then I met Mr. Missigman who even got one up on Mr. Libby. They talked back and forth much like two martial artists sparring with one another and trying to see who could get the best technique in on the other. Both wearing hearing aids and interjecting comments at the same time was quite a comical thing to try and follow as well. As one woud start a story and proceed, half way through, the other would start their own all-the-while I was trying to direct the camera to the one that was either talking the loudest or who won that round and was given the chance to finish their memory of the war. At one point, Mr. Missigman left the room and Mr. Libby looked at me and said . . .

```
      "Boy, he really likes to talk. I can't get a
      word in edge-wise!"
```

I smiled and thought to myself, a true opponent for Mr. Libby in the realm of story-telling. As he came back to talk some more, the two sat on the couch together and began to share locations that both remembered seeing or staying during that time. Mr. Missigman even shared some stories that enabled us to piece together some of the locations and landmarks that Mr. Libby had mentioned in our interviews that helped me in the writing of this book. He took a jab at Mr. Libby with the humorous comment during a story Mr. Libby was telling along the lines of *"You are full of it, I know about all you tank guys."* when speaking about the women of France.

We all got a big laugh out of it and they continued their story swapping.

We also learned during our talks that Mr. Missigman traveled back to France with President Ronald Reagen to aid in the planning of several WWII memorials and also attended many other important functions and ceremonies long after WWII. He participated in many things after the war that helped the US in their honoring of the men and women who served, fought and died during this time of war. This soft-spoken man lived just a few minutes from my own home and I never knew what type of national treasure was there with these stories and important information tucked away in his brain.

Upon further discussion, he revealed to us that he was the man that prepared the two bodies that were placed within the *Tomb of the Unknown Soldier* as well as preparing the body of General George S. Patton *himself* for burial. That was one that even got Mr. Libby excited and impressed him greatly! Truly a remarkable man and an equally remarkable day for both myself and Mr. Libby to experiece. It was a big treat for me to have the ability to sit with these two heroes of WWII and to also have the video to watch and remember that occasion.

Mr. Missigman shook our hands on the way out the door and told us to come back any time that we wanted. With my handshake, he looked at me and spoke softly . . .

"Let me know when you are ready to do some more writing."

I believed at the time that he meant to come back and spend time listening to his stories and to write a book based upon his life and time spent performing his duties in WWII. I spent the next several months staying focused on this project for Mr. Libby and before I knew it, Mr. Missigman passed away taking many of the stories with him from that great era of history. I regret not working faster, but do have the great memory of that one meeting. On September 24, 2014, at the age of 96, Mr. Charles Missigman joined all of those boys who he spent time preparing to be sent back home to their families. He joined them in a very special place with The Lord in heaven for all the unselfish and tireless work he endured putting his emotions aside and doing the job that the US government asked of him. *Nobody* could have expected to do what was asked of him and for that, we honor him within this story as one of the important puzzle pieces in the grand scheme and story of WWII. RIP Mr. Missigman and thank you so much for your service to our country and it's many citizens as well as verification on some important facts within my manuscript about Mr. Libby. God Bless You!

A Note and Disclaimer from the Author

✳ ✳ ✳

THE STORIES WRITTEN IN THIS manuscript are entirely from the memories of Mr. Charles A. Libby. In staying true to these memories, I used names and events that have been locked away in his memories for many, many years. With a tremendous recall of these events, I did have some difficulty at times piecing together a time-line which matches some of the written historical events of this time. I am not a historian by any means. Again, in staying true to his recall, Mr. Libby had his personal duties and jobs as an orderly and as a command car driver which may have been different from that of the main unit at times and in these places. These duties led him into places that others didn't go or places that events occurred that were not under the microscope of onlookers or that of any type of formal military recorded documentation.

Written history is just that, a written account of moments, happenings and truths that occurred either with or without witnesses to back up the complete and true story. In many cases within this book, the witnesses are no longer living. At the age of 97, Mr. Libby has outlived many of these people in these written accounts. In my mind, they are all true and without any type selfishness or with any malice. The man who endured these events in Europe during WWII wanted to share these stories to give others a taste of what he saw, smelled, felt and witnessed without any intent of changing the most accurate of details. My interpretation of the stories by adding my own dialogue was to help to bring the images alive within your mind as you read his incredible stories. It is my hope that I achieved this and also my hope that you enjoy my writing style.

In many cases, I truly believe that history may have been written to sway opinion of the times or to add a touch of romanticism to an already unbelievable series of events. Therefore, as the author, I submit these stories as an amendment to the already written and widely accepted interpretations of the modern history of WWII. Please accept these stories as new information gathered by a person that actually witnessed it first-hand. As we advance through time, details become buried, destroyed or forgotten. We are also seeing today, the political correctness and the selfish pursuit to try and make others believe that events either didn't happen or the truth behind some of the events and symbols are full of hatred, which is in most cases, is not true. The thin-skinned society which we live in should embrace history the way it was, good or bad and either strive to keep it's memory alive as a tribute to it's greatness or to learn from it in a way as not to ever repeat it, but *never* try to hide it from future generations. It is with great pride that I dig up, restore and help to bring into the spotlight new details so that they do not become forgotten events from this amazing time in our written history.

Mr. Libby faced a tremendous strain on his emotions several times during these long interviews in remembering some of these painful events. There were several occasions that we were both found at the work station in tears. He also dialed into the more pleasurable events with enthusiasm and great zeal as he told those particular stories. Tremendous discipline was required on his part to slow down the *faucet of information* once it was opened and tremendous discipline was required by this author to know when to say, "*Tell me more or that's enough for today.*"

It has been a unique experience as well as a tremendous honor to associate with Mr. Libby and to capture these memories within my mind which I will carry with me for the rest of my life. I find myself wishing that I had known the people who he spoke of or had been there to witness the events that he lived.

This is another reason why writers take on the challenge of writing books for others to read, because we can't be everywhere, we can't go back in time and we can't often fathom the events spoken by those who were there and experienced it.

During my work in the preparation of this book, I found myself so enthralled by the stories that I myself had intense dreams of the events and happenings during my limited sleep. One particular night I was placed back in time watching Mr. Libby from a position behind his Command Car as he drove through the streets of a town which was under attack. Mr. Libby was avoiding the incoming small arms fire and the mortars that were hitting on all sides of him. Looking back, I believe that my mind placed me in heat of *The Battle of the Bulge*. I witnessed several German foot soldiers coming to the left side of his vehicle from a ditch who I intercepted before they could reach him. I woke myself up from my deep and intense sleep by yelling out to Mr. Libby to watch out for these attacking soldiers. This is a testament to the level of overall commitment that I had while preparing this book. This happened to me several times and made me think about the soldiers that *actually lived it*! The dreams that haunt them, the long sleepless nights and the feeling that they *never* actually left there. My heart goes out to all of them.

Until such time as Mr. Libby passes on and joins our Lord in Heaven, I am sure that many more events and stories will continue to flow from his memories. I am sure that the faucet of information will continue to stay open and details will unfold long after this book is published. It is my hope and goal to continue to stay focused on his stories and to continue to document them until that time arrives. In hopes of bringing these many stories to the masses, I am sure that the desire to know more and more about this particular war and the events that surrounded it will become an unquenchable thirst for many. There will be a time when it all will be written and a time when there are *no more* witnesses to these events and a time when the chapters are closed, all books have been written and all that will remain will be conclusions made by people as to how and what happened to the entire world during these years carved out in time. I proudly offer this manuscript as a *missing puzzle piece* that can now be inserted into the correct hole or position within the bigger picture that will someday be a finished product. Enjoy and God Bless!

A young Charles Libby having fun with the camera operator during his time on US maneuvers.

About the Author

✶ ✶ ✶

STEVE HUNTER AND HIS FAMILY are residents of South Williamsport, Pennsylvania. Steve considers himself to be a multi-faceted artist. His main profession is as an entertainer. He owns his own company which provides musical entertainment for many different occasions. His family incorporates music from the early eras of recording into a Christian ministry that tours the many nursing homes and health care facilities around the state of Pennsylvania. Their vocal performances known as *"Music With The Hunters"*, brings happiness to those who are either in their final days or those who have made these facilities their final home on their journey.

Hunter has studied the martial arts most of his life and made a full-time career of it from 1986 until his recent retirement from operating dojos in 2011. Hunter, an 8th degree martial arts master, has been published world-wide in several martial arts publications. Recognized in the *Who's Who of the Martial Arts*, he has had a full career of both competing and training others in this valuable art form. He still heads up the Buke-ryu Martial Arts Federation and teaches seminars for the many who study this art as well as the authorizing of any and all black belt promotions within this style of martial arts he created and is recognized within the traditional martial arts community.

In 2012, Hunter penned a book and self-published this now world-wide publication entitled "**Training Heroes**." Hunter speaks on this book at signings and hopes to continue his writing career far past this newest writing project along with future speaking events and projects that bring both happiness to others as well as preserving history for future generations to enjoy and to learn from.

Hunter enjoys his inherit rights to go into the many types of outdoors that this country provides and harvest meat for his family. His passion for this lifestyle of hunting and survival has led him to a project that he hopes will offer a future television show on this subject by incorporating these principles and training of the martial arts as well as a Christian approach to his many art forms. Hunting provides this author with quiet time to create, design and write. These times spent alone in the thick northern woods and mountains as well as the southern scenderos, gives Hunter time to pray and ask for guidance and creativity. He would like to encourage others to help to preserve this activity for future generations in any way possible and to enjoy the many blessings that are available all year long!

Hunter can be reached by e-mail at : shihanhunter@yahoo.com for any comments, discussions, questions and for bookings in any of the fields that he provides services including speeches, appearances, book signings, martial arts seminars and musical shows. **Steve Hunter** can also be found on the popular social media site *Facebook* at the following page locations :

Steve.hunter.792@facebook.com

From The Command Car at : www.facebook.com/fromthecommandcar

Web Site Address : www.fromthecommandcar.com

Training Heroes at : www.facebook.com/shihanhunter

Sponsors Of History

✶ ✶ ✶

THE FOLLOWING INDIVIDUALS, GROUPS, BUSINESSES and historical organizations are all proud to have donated to and sponsor this written piece of history. Their understanding of this process and the great efforts taken to preserve such stories is appreciated by both myself as the author and by Mr. Charles Libby. God bless you and thank you all for your kindness, help and your generosity!

OFFICIAL SPONSORSHIP PRESERVATION MEMBERS
Rick and Linda Cowden
Monica Diltz and The Brass Pelican Restaurant – Benton, PA
Ruth Rode
Daughters and Family of Irene Seward Lechleitner
The Tivoli United Methodist Church Christian Ladies Group
Tivoli, PA
Melanie and Wylie Norton
Timothy and Nancy Hampton
The Sullivan County Historical Society Museum
458 Meylert Street   Laporte, PA   18626
www.scpahistory.com

Additional Membership Preservation Members
Marie and Willard Cressman
Irvin and Margaret V. Fox
The Union County Library – Lewisburg, PA

Special Thanks For Additional Help

Bill Williams	Dave & Ellen Machmer
James Dortman	Patsy Truskoloski
Glenda Lechleitner	Deb Stackhouse
Meg Geffken	Cara Morningstar

Mr. Charles Missigman
The Williamsport Sun-Gazette
Jack Craft and Endless Mt. Museum – Sonestown, PA
and
All that attended the speeches that we presented along the path to the publishing of this book.

Special Thanks To
Jody Harlan for her talent in providing my author photo!

www.ingramcontent.com/pod-product-compliance
Lightning Source LLC
Chambersburg PA
CBHW060500090426
42735CB00011B/2051